Full of humor, truth, anger, and tenderness . . . Rosellen Brown has given us a novel stripped down to essences in this remarkable set of poems, the vivid evocations of a country woman's life.

—May Sarton

In *Cora Fry's Pillow Book* Rosellen Brown returns to Oxford, New Hampshire, to discover what has changed and what has stayed the same for Cora Fry, her family, and her friends after nearly twenty years. In a voice that speaks to us all, these poems confront the challenges that come with a woman's growth toward middle age: Cora's children are now adults; her parents and friends present a series of bewildering, sometimes painful dilemmas; and her relations with men reflect a seasoned understanding. Yet Cora manages to find some redemption, comfort, even wry humor in any circumstance. Once a waitress and now a rural mail carrier, Cora Fry is one of the "unbreakable threads" that hold her small-town community together. And now the danger to her place in the world, and the role of her small town, comes from outside forces. A poignant exploration of family, love, and loyalty, *Cora Fry's Pillow Book* includes the entire text of *Cora Fry*.

Rosellen Brown is the author of four novels, *Before and After*, *Civil Wars*, *Tender Mercies*, and *The Autobiography of My Mother*; a book of stories, *Street Games*; and a volume of poems, *Some Deaths in the Delta*. She teaches writing at the University of Houston, and lives in Houston, Texas.

T0057976

CORA FRY'S

PILLOW BOOK

CORA FRY'S

PILLOW BOOK

ROSELLEN BROWN

FARRAR STRAUS GIROUX

NEW YORK

Library of Congress Cataloging-in-Publication Data
Brown, Rosellen.
Cora Fry's pillow book / Rosellen Brown
p.   cm.
1. City and town life—New Hampshire—Poetry.   2. Women—New
Hampshire—Poetry.   I. Title.
PS3552.R7C63   1994   811'.54—dc20   94-14729   CIP

Author photo © 1994 by Jerry Bauer

This is for both generations—

for my mother, Blossom

and my daughters, Adina and Elana

Contents

CORA FRY

I want to understand light-years.
I live in Oxford, New Hampshire.
When, then, will the light get to me?

The year I die
there'll be no snow.

Look, Nan, the
first shy snow

half falling.
Like moths I

shook out once
from a coat:

they fell down
slowly, so

slowly, and
some woke up

halfway out
into the air.

The rest fell
to the floor

still folded.

Nan, do you think moths dream?

All the men
are on the plows.
It's snowing up-
side down now.

My father
runs this show.
Here he comes, slow,
riding high,
a roar, a
yellow eye
in the ice-fog.

Some men hate him
good. But his
followers
follow in his
slippery footsteps
casting salt,
snow on snow,

December
manna.

I.

"Fry," I said
when he touched me on
my breast. "Do you think
of women,
other women, when
you're touching me there?"

In the dark
I could feel him blink—
butterfly
kiss like I give Nan
on the cheek.
"Sometimes," he said, "sort
of to crank
it up." He half-shrugged
but couldn't move much.
"Don't worry,"
and put his mouth there.
"No one you know."

II.

I thought I'd
try it too. I made
a dozen
faces come bend down
to kiss me,
all neighbors and Frank
from work—but
scared, I turned my head
so hard Fry
said "Hey kid,
should I go brush my teeth
again?" I
gave my mouth to him
and saw black.
It takes something I don't have
and don't want. So it's Fry now
forever.

I go on Sunday
for some mystery.
But Reverend Merman
takes my hand and milks
it like an udder.
I blame myself but
at the door he dries
me out until I
crack. Gossip seeps in,
face powder, after-
shave, sermon on hope,
oh Merman, mermaid,
I give a dollar
(what with inflation
that saves half a soul)
and the hymn. Jesus
himself could sit down
beside me here and
find me out to lunch:

Chicken. Rice. Green peas.

One bad winter
my father poached
a deer and I died

thousands of hard
separate deaths
waiting for the

sheriff to come.
The blue light swung
across my wall

one snowbound night.
I stopped breathing.
I woke up Sam.

But it was just
the deputy,
fat Lloyd the tease,

coming to get
Daddy, his plow
and all, to pull

some foreign car
out of his field.
"Some kid got throwed

clear in a bank,
but he hit hard."
I clamored till

I got to come,
in Dad's army
blanket, shivering.

The boy was still
lying in blue
shadows, his arms

out like a snow
angel. He woke
after a while,

blood in his mouth,
swearing he had
only one beer.

The sheriff laughed
and winked at us.
Lloyd muttered "Bull . . ."

Quarter to four
on a moony
night in late March

I swallowed hard
and the deer went down.

I saw Chickering Webb today.
He put his whole hand on my thigh
once in the high school library.
I kept smiling and took it off.
That was the day before he went
crazy, and holed up in a house
with Judy Carney. Poor Miss Sleigh,
it was her house they chose to have
their orgy in. They defamed all
her father's books (Earl Sleigh the judge),
they gummed the walls with Crisco and
they gashed the sheets and cracked her bed.
Nobody ever said Judy
went crazy too. She wouldn't press
charges or tell us anything.

Chip thinks people stop
when he can't see them.

The summer people
load their cars and go
out of Oxford's sight,
far out of mind—though
every December
the Johns send a card
crammed with skyscrapers
and lit store windows
to whet my envy.
This year a tiny
car dragged a huge tree
through downtown traffic.

It's a game we play,
postmark to postmark.
Fist raised against fist.
For Oxford this year,
I sent a single star.

When the snow
got up to the window frame,
grainy as
sugar, each crystal a face
in a crowd
and the crowd silent for death,

do you know,
I wanted a field pale green
with sheep sorrel—
warm and sour,
those light clover heads shaking,
"Everything's shaggy, newborn. Lie down here
and eat me!"

What are friends for, my mother asks.
A duty undone, visit missed,
casserole unbaked for sick Jane.
Someone has just made her bitter.

Nothing. They are for nothing, friends,
I think. All they do in the end—
they *touch* you. They fill you like music.

The moonless night
the ice hill
the snow without shadows

are mine because
I need them.
I drive down the long slope

in first, waiting
to lose hold
and slip to the bottom.

They'll find the car
pulverized
and my shadow for shame.

But it all holds:
luck, gears—sand
to the stop sign.
Bless the sweet town grit!

Joe Fox
sent his kids away
to school.
I think
if they'd been some way
special—
too smart
or sick or dumb . . .
To me,

Joe said,
they're special: they're mine.
Then what
the hell
does that make mine, asked
Father.
Makes 'em
yours, I guess, said Joe.

Sam beat
the buttons off Tom's coat
for that,
and I
loved Meg so much I
stuck my
tongue out
at her for a month.
Cut her,

Cut her,
Father taunted,

see if
she bleeds
red or white or
don't you think it's
blue now?

I go to work because it pays.
I go to work to get away.
I go to work to change my face.
I go to work to wash my hands
and wear a wig to save my head.
(I leave mine home.)
I go to work to be unknown
and in the kitchen sweating rain
I put a heavy tray down full

and watch the new man watching me.
What messages between his eyes
and mine there's room for here. . . . He's thin
as someone's undernourished son.
If I go ask for some glasses,
depending on my voice and where
my shoulders are, compared to his,
I could make room on his pillow
for my head, with or without wig.
I move my tray the other way.

Felice moves then, smiling her gap-
tooth grin. Her thighs, I think, open
and close, mouth breathing mostly in,
chattering at men endlessly,
wanting to be shut, not sweetly.

Felice has stopped two babies quick.
Times she thought they were taking care.
"Don't trust them, Core, with a blind nun.
They could care less. No matter how
they watch your ass, it's yours to watch."

The salesmen's convention
means ass cooked to order,
complained about, drinks spilled,
can't I sit on their lap,
see what they've got for me,
"a very special tip."

I put tapioca
and coffee down, smiling,
smiling as if I'm deaf
until I hear this one
shark-shouldered manager
lean to his friend and say
"That Billie Holiday,
before she got big-league,
some café in Harlem,
brought change between her *lips*.
And I don't mean her mouth,
pal, I don't mean her mouth."

I slam his second cup
of coffee, not well aimed—
I'd love to singe his lap
so he'll see purple pain
next time he gets it up
for waitress, wife, or whore.
It splashes on his cuff.
I'll live without his tip.

Nan curled in my lap.
Look at the picture: spaghetti legs!
I think I was happiest right then,
when she pulled my breasts
right inside out, like party favors . . .

■

"That's what they're for, Nan,"
I tell her when Chip pats them gently.
When she needs to know
I'll warn her men only think they own
your breasts. When Fry bends
to them, sometimes it feels like Nanny
or Chip, and I cry.
"Did I hurt you, hon?" he'll say. I swear
they let down milk for him.

The flowers won't grow
in the north window.

Grandmother Rule
I know went mad.
She starved to bone
and broke herself.

Mother says all
the women in
the family do,
this way or that,

which leaves some room
for Nan and me.
When it comes time
to read her will

we'll pick our pain
slowly and well:
the family jewel.

The closets are going to explode.
The table is going to collapse.
The sink is sinking.
The door just slams and slams.
The baby's crying, where's his sister?
Don't jump on me, my bones are empty.
My joints are being washed and ironed.
I'm getting an extra hour of sleep.
Before there is no more to heal up,
I'm taking the cure: *I pass. I pass.*

Fry says a word
in my poor ear
I could do with-
out. In the dark
all of me frowns.
He'll be sorry
when he gets there.

Reverend Merman
tried to convince us
only the seasons
are real. They *prevail*,
is how he said it.
And, friends, they *triumph*.

They do. But meanwhile—
what a bother—here
we are. Here I am.
Rain's in the bucket,
cow's in the pea patch,
the pigs want dinner
and so do the kids.

I think I'll tell them
when winter prevails
on them, they won't be
hungry anymore:

they'll be snowchildren
in the great triumph
of time over tooth
and nail. I'll tell them,
Go melt on God's fool.

I watch my cousin Valerie
who lives at the top of Brick Hill,
riding Sim's arm, smiling, smiling.
She's young, it's enough just to find
some dark place to lie down with him,
no steering wheel, no mosquitoes,
and know that everybody knows.
She listens to him talk football.
She prods him and laughs a little.

Doesn't she know the end's written?
When he sees her lie in the light,
finds one hair under her nipple,
she's got her Tupperware together,
he puts his ear to her swollen
belly for the first child only.
He says she was a good listener,
he watches the ball come toward him
out of the snow of the TV,
he catches it. Now it's the ball
of his gut, tight with fries and beer.

After her third the doctor winks:
"I took that husband-stitch for you,
dear." He thinks that's what holds husbands,
the tuck he takes in the yard goods.
He's a husband, doesn't he know
they want to graze in new meadow?
What holds them is what lets them go.

The diving crew
is under ice.
My father says
muffled goodbyes,
walks to the hole
and disappears.

We stand knotted
in a corner
of the wind-wall,
away from the
mother whose child
stiffens far down
in a stone shroud.

We don't know her,
this visitor
who brought her son
for evergreens
and frozen ponds,
a white Christmas
up in Oxford.

We only hear
her voice rising
to beat against
the wind's sharp wall.

Bubbles rise. My
silver father
stands dripping ice.
Shaking he spits
the child out whole,
and then he cries.

That table:
white oblong
blue-bordered
enamel,
chipped and clean.
Hit it right
with a spoon,
it rang out
loud for you.

Our kitchen's
all in it.
'45?
'48?
The baking—
the bread pail
hitched on tight,
screwed with that
big silver
butterfly;
me cranking
our breakfast
for the week.
The turkey
set on its
buttered rear
like a dog
met with an
accident.
The berries
giving up
their hard stems.
My homework

Mama cleaned
all around
with her rag.

Her housedress—
pink and green.
Bobby sox;
Mother in
red loafers;
me with my
winking dimes.

Sentiment
hides under
the blue rim
out of sight
like chewed gum.
Was it mine,
that childhood?
Sweet and soft. . . .
Now see me
saving it,
even when
it gets too
hard to chew.

Did you know during
the Second World War

they turned the lights out
"in the country" too,

and listened for planes
roaring in German?

Even New Hampshire
had targets, though God

only knows which hill
we thought they wanted.

I was a child called
Cora Pearl Hubberd

you could hear crying
all over town,

shamelessly. I thought
I was about to

die. Nothing fancy:
just die in the dark
of war, of missing
my father.

■

My cousin Norb died in a tree
by sniper fire in Anzio.
I always pictured a monkey

and in my head changed the subject,
that was so disrespectful.

All I remembered of Norbert
from Keene, smart enough for glasses,
was how he peed in the bushes
visiting us when he was twelve.
How when he pulled his zipper up
he said, "Don't look at me like that.
Sometimes a man has got no choice."

I was staring hard at his face
that was very blond and pink veined
to keep from watching how his hands
tugged and propped up and then tucked back
the intricate thing he carried
sheathed, the way my brother hid his.

Worse than the monkey, when I heard
he died I saw his silver arc
that spattered on the day lilies
saying NORBERT WAS HERE and gone.

All the places
I've never been

                Minnesota
                Greenwich Village
                Daytona Beach

I don't really
want to go there

                but just to see
                how people look

with thousands of
grandmothers from
                foreign countries
                (none in English)

Would the difference
(Mother says yes)
make me nervous?

My father
says choice rots
the bones like
candy rots
the teeth.

I have a neighbor
who is always deep
in a book or two.

High tides of clutter
rise in her kitchen.

Which last longer, words,
words in her bent head,
or the clean spaces

between one perfect
dusting and the next?

Up to East
Oxford, the distant cousins

of rich men
live scratching in their good names

right on the
blacktop shoulder where all the

action is.
NIGHT CRAWLERS   BODY WORK   BRAKES

DRINK FRESCA
Their trailers rust. Their old cars

stand grazing
like horses put to pasture.

Chip runs like a squirrel
his cowlick   his tail

■

And Nan is old
enough to smile
like a daughter-
in-arms. Secret.
No teeth showing.

■

They do gnaw me
sometimes.
Their voices grind
fine, my
thumbs, my liver.

I can't
be a weapon,
it would
be too easy
to pinch, to kill,
to say
some word they won't
forget.

And if I died
would they
remember me
shouting?

Fry's hands have life lines
traced black to the bone.
He rests them against
my weak-white shoulder
and I shouldn't wilt.

Fry who walks through worlds
I can barely see,
fixing things that have
no voices: Brakes.
Clocks.
They're the animals
he feeds tenderly
or gives a light shove
to ease their movement.

On the bureau now
our old healed clock glows
under its warm skin.

You can do
anything alone
anything but
laugh out loud

We watch them hoist a streetlamp
over the bridge at the brook.
The stiff crane squeaks and lunges.

Why do we need a night light?
The dark outside my bedroom
is the safest dark there is:
sweet-smelling, familiar.
Glow worms wink up from the road
after rain. The moon comes back
and it shines like melting ice.

Now I study hard shadows
that were never there before.
I wait for someone to bolt
out of the light toward my door.

Coming home late from work,
I stopped the car one long thirsty minute
on the hilltop near my father's meadow.

Something plunged and tossed in the center
like a show animal in a lit ring.

He threw his head, he shook it free of air,
his legs flung whichway. There were the antlers,
a forest of spring twigs that rose and dived,
dancing. *Singing,* for all I knew, glassed in.

I rolled my window down
knowing I'd lose him, and I did: he ducked
into nowhere. But I had that one glimpse,

didn't I, of the animal deep in
the animal? Of his freedom flaring

only a quick blink of light? I think spring
must be a crazy water animals drink.

I used to
play here but
the field was
so much bigger

I squint to understand
how they can make bombs
of themselves, and light them.

Think. Think. Your child is dead,
someone's to blame.
You watch a bottle hit

the school bus. Your house burns
on purpose. You're a doll
the whole world sticks pins in.

The ones who need vengeance
are not the avengers—
only their kid brothers.

(Our yellow bus blurs by,
stops in its wide green frame:
Nan's head bobs to its place
at the door. She's home free.)

Fry says they just do it
to terrify their mothers.

In this sun
the wood grain
of the shed
is water.
The whole wall
is water.

Pretend to
throw a stone.
Watch it sink,
rippling out
from the hollow
heartwood.

Up the road over Snow Brook
our nearest neighbors Mister
and Mrs. Thaddeus Cole
at home in the steep brick house

look down on us from so high
you'd think they lived on a cliff.

I met her on the creek bridge.
Would I clean her house, she begged,
only so nice, no nicer?

"Can you see lady's slippers
behind that rock?" I asked her.
She never moved her coiled head.
"They look like tongues, not slippers!"
Then Nan came along dirty
on her bike and Mrs. Cole
looked sick. "Good morning," she said,

and went back up the blacktop
to her peonies and her rooms
full of good help, satisfied.

Nan goes to the cemetery
with her class: with that young teacher.
Two by two they paper the old
stones, tape over the brittleness,
turn their Crayolas flat side up
(peeled back to the orange and purple),
and rub until the facts take shape
under their innocent fingers.

(Wives to both sides of the CAPTAIN,
who outlived even his MOTHER.
And the little bastard called JAS.
outside the limits of the yard,
no coarser ash than his judges.)

"I've got a baby!" my Nan squeals.
Delight. "What do you think killed it?"
Horror tickles her. She bends down.
The blunt carved face is like a slate
frog, crude as though the child worked it
herself. *LYDIA ANN Returned*
How well I remember that one,
I spent such years on my scuffed knees
worshipping true love, true loss, gone,
hardened, all of it, to mossed stone.

Like a blind child, Nan feels the dates.
She twitches fingers, counting up.
Soon she'll get to the hardest part
"wonder drugs" and "hygiene" can't stop:
that Lydia Ann would be dead now
no matter what. No matter *what*.

The mailman, Drew Teague,
puts his wheels against
my petunias thick
as faces crowding
around the mailbox.
He tugs the rusty
door open and squints
inside: no red flag
means no mail to go.
Listen to me, Drew,
if I had something
to write to someone
well out of earshot
I'd put your flag up,
call to you, *Toro!*
What's happened today
that's worth a postcard?

You bring me two bills,
an ad for snow tires,
and a letter from
my brother who is
famous nowadays
for living with a
girl named Fran in sin
at a safe distance
"to hurt his mother"
where such things are done.
Oh, he's coming home.
I mean, they are.
Well. He'll turn to me,
Sam will, and, smiling,

forgive *me,* his eyes
wide to take me in.

I would have lived with
no one but my books.
The men in old books.
Even they would need
to struggle to get
a smile from me, let
alone much more. Sam
introduced me once
to someone who said
"Smile, you're on *Candid
Camera!"* and I did.
But he didn't; he
left the way I think
men also leave when
they have made you smile
wide everywhere. I
never lived in sin
or even mischief.

Now when I do dream
of luscious freedom
it's not to be needed.
To be just alone . . .

Muskrat, Muskrat.
Trapped at the tooth-
pick ankle, when
you pull you are
raking yourself
to the soft dark
center. You gouge
your groin with what
edges you find—
can opener,
stone-lip, blunt flint,
what's the difference,
they're all like teeth.
You saw, you chew,
forward and back,
raising a smoke-
trail, hot, quiet,
over your head.
A snarl: come free
you roll, hobble,
you start a new
life on three legs.

Big game-hunters
Chip and Craig Fry,
checking the trap,
will pick your leg up,
shake it, bloody
knotted short string
trailing a rag
of web, and curse
you. "Double cross."

(Fry to his son,
angry. Chip pouts
to please his dad.)

Fry cracks your bone,
wishbone easy
in his tight fist.
The leg sails, lands
on leaves, becomes
a crooked twig,
or an inchworm.
They turn to lunch.

In my kitchen,
blotting water
stains off the forks,
the child-safe knives,
I can see you:

By now you are
under the cliff,
under the mountain,
eating your pain.

Linda Swain, my old friend,
at the gas pump gazing—
gazing's the word—across
Route 8 to the graveyard.

Why has her long sweet hair
gone gray like my mother's?
Why haven't I seen her
for years? I look right through
the Class of '61
as though we're made of glass.

Linda was getting out
but, first mistake, she let
Tom in. She's pumping gas
for him. He lets her crawl
under a car sometimes
(hooray for women's lib)
and drain the sludgy oil
into the common pail.

From the far, the graveyard, side
I watch her with my arms
full of DUBL-STRENGTH bags
(milk, Kool-Aid, and cat food).
We're two small girls who aren't
allowed to cross ourselves.

We found the gravestone
of the first mistress
of a quarter of this house.

Her quarter would have been fire-
place and keeping-room.
This was the barnyard.
Sitting right here, see
my old maple hers, and young,
and this stump with its hundred
pale rings in full-shadowed blossom.

Where I sip iced tea
she spun wool and wove
with her competent daughters,
and pushed her needle.
I do complain and mope
too much, Mistress Jonah Hoyt.
I do. I turn the channel
to strangers' angers.

Because I see such others
you never heard of,
and they make me want.
Because they drag their empty
afternoons and full evenings
across my vision, I want.

Is it all the same,
life measured by love
in spoonfuls, silver
or soft Woolworth tin?

Never more hard nor easy?
What did you covet?

If you had three good chickens
you were envied a season.
Did you keep your waist?
Did you go to Boston?
Did your children live?
Imagine the breasts
of the young mother of eight—
long and veined with blue—
mirrored in her husband's eyes
that he remembered
when he went for a soldier . . .

In the long grasses
that soaked the hem of your dress,
in Captain Hoyt's high bedstead
receiving a child
in modest silence,
did you do better
than tolerate yourself?

Carrots and peas, beans and brussels sprouts,
they all go into the ground on cue
from the feel of the air, soft evenings.
I come out right with the mourning dove,
his loony alto song; bend spotting
where the tiny bright identical
double wings poke up out of thick dirt.
Each year I doubt, each year they prosper.
I soothe their rows with tepid water,
I tend their margins, tuck and pull up,
housekeep the wildness where I may, so

when our woodchuck comes, he has his feast
neat as a salad.
                              I will not use
Fry's .22. He says I'd rather
buy my greens at the A & P and
look at my shorn rows like a mother
who's lost her children to the plague,
and cry.

Last night I had this dream:

I didn't mark the rows
and where I planted chard
and trusted it would grow
without a sign to tell
it how,

       a mass of flesh,
veiny and deep, with hair
matted like something smashed,
hunched waiting in the row.

I turned it with my shoe
and it rolled to the light:
infant faces swarming
with those lip-colored worms
that say your soil is good.

I will not forgive Fry
planting that dream in me.

Chip, remember this
always—how you thought
the merry-go-round
would take you away,
the red and white horse
canter off across
the town green. How you
stood in the stirrups
calling "Goodbye! Goodbye,
Mommy!", crying
and waving, but brave,
going. Holding on.

When you saw me come
round the second time,
I got to see your face.

Slipping
between the cool sheets of the
water

I am concentrating
on the lives of squashes:

the St. Pat scallop, thick
and placid, a ruffled
pale girl in baby fat.
This slick zucchini, striped,
clever, the racing car
of squashes, the greyhound.
And here the zeppelin,
my pale blue Hubbard pumped
with nothing like hot air.
Hiding among their wild
leaves turned up like human
palms, their toothed stems that bite,
they love to surprise me.

How does a family
of nine hundred cousins
survive in such cool peace,
such silence? I hold them
in my apron still warm.

I catch the tomato,
haul it out of water,
strip it down quick to soft
flesh, oozing hard gold seeds,
drop it through the fat neck
of the bottle. It spreads
haunches with its sisters,
settling in sheer bubbles,
softening in itself.

These days I could buy cans.
I can't. I love the fat
human sprawl of the fruit
slipping through my fingers,
the patient shelf keeping
till deep January;
then opening up the seal
on the best day of summer.

This is no baby skin—
Chip?
You are a new apple.
If
I take a healthy bite
I
get to the star of seeds,
right?

I'm leaving.
Say goodbye
to mother.

Gone fishing
said Mister
Man, you go

to sleep and
don't wait up.
Where is he?

Slip around,
I can see
that happens

(though not to
Fry and me.
He *never*.)

But to go
with these friends
I don't know,

new around—
beer guzzlers,
baby wives—

to Boston—
some Red Sox—
red *garters,*

maybe. And
come home dead
in the legs,

in the eyes,
smelling like
Tillie's rose.

Go away
Fry, I said.
Go lie down

overnight
with Carl Yaz,
wake up late,

roll her back,
say hello
from Cora.

Put it there, country.
When you go
leave a ten
on the bureau.

You are not
my husband.

I hit the tree
at thirty.
It came toward me
and I saw the bark,
long finger-scratches
down its back.

■

No ambulance
no scrooo-reee   go
get the road clear
for here comes   who

Tom Fox found me
his cruiser slammed
its wheels right up
I hurt the tree

not a word Tom   not
a blessed word
Poor Cora   he
whispered and my

fingers loosened
on the steering
wheel   I bit down
on blood   on his

tinfoil shield   his
tongue going *Poor
Cora   Poor Cora*

Cora Fry
I said.
I do not want to die.
I am not dead.

I only need—
What did he say?
I want to see
him cry.

■

My white gown
parts in back.
No one can see
my devil cleft.
No one will ever
have to touch me
anywhere
again. I'm free.

■

They can
put you back together
but you
see   you come in small parts.
If there's
one missing   some big one
then they send to
Boston   but they might not
have it

I wouldn't feel this way because of "sex."

"Sex" just comes and goes
like sap running up and down a maple.
And men, my mother
always knew, have no
control, out the spile the sap comes running.
Sometimes when it boils it can even be sweet.

It isn't the vow
that I thought he meant.
But doesn't he owe
me more at home, here in the hand-built bed
where he won't let me read
because of the light,
on the sheets I bleach,
in the room I dust,

than he owes those men?
But Fry's a pal,
one of the fast boys all of a sudden.
They laughed about us
going to Boston—
"a night off the old
lady"—"the dead wood!"
while our ears burned red,
me and their kid wives here for the having.

The "sex" I forgive.
It was the laughing.

Mother said "Marriage
is like driving a
car. All you can do
is worry about
yourself. You can't stay
wide-awake sober
for somebody else,
or keep him on the
right side of the road."

The neighbors listened
all unvisited
in their quiet beds.

"I make the whole bed,
Mother, not my side."

She shook her head, tired.
I have brought her shame—
not that my husband
cheats but that I bruise
so easily.

Who digs her old car
up to its fenders
into an oak tree
and gets dragged out mad,
not even sorry?

"Well, you'll never know
the things I could tell."

"What can you tell me?"

My mother looks down
onto her used breasts.
Her ankles are soft,
her legs lavender.

"Women are boring,
Cora. Every month
they make the same mess.
Every wedding day
sign the same bargain.

We all lie right down
under a ton weight
and then we can't move.
And then we're surprised.
Well, what can you think
but we deserve it?"

On the next bed floats
the lacy remains
of a grand old dame
eaten like a shawl
by famished white moths.
She has their moth-voice.

The farmer's wife nods,
nods in her fat. Hair
decorates her face,
chin whiskers. All wrong,
her signals got mixed,

all wrong. She is her
husband now. He wastes,
still wanting a wife.

We are not boring,
Ma. We are just drilled
with imperfections:
holes and moles and eyes

to watch, retreating,
the same backs over
and over. Maybe
the ones who leave us—
husbands, children, cats—
maybe they're the ones
who make me yawn: left
foot in front of right
plodding to freedom.

I'll bet they're even
boring to God who
sees their backs as often
as any ordinary woman.

Trundling home
from the hospital
light-headed
gasping in the sun

(Remember
Nan fresh in my arms
sexless in
her yellow blanket
I stood on
this hospital porch
drinking light
with my own new eyes)

Widowed now
by my own fury
buried to the waist
in bad blood

the hinges of my
thighs will rust

The weekend shift.
Work keeps me clean.
All the faces
I am smiling
at are strangers.
Some smile back, some
yell like husbands.
I take a towel
and scrub my hands
clean for the health
department, clean
for my conscience
like a good girl
before dinner.
Father used to
review my nails
and then say grace.
I go out front
with a full tray,
plastic woman
cool to the touch
in the brisk wig
Fry despises.

In the cloakroom
while I'm working,
my confusion
curls in my coat
pocket like a
smooth snail, also
cool to the touch,
soft parts drawn in.

On my break I
finger it. Go
out there to touch
pity, my small stone.

The man smells some desperation.
Frank stacks the dishwasher full
to overflowing and turns
to slow me down with his eyes.

Do I wear pain like a wild slash
across my cheek? Does he know
I'm thinking of giving up
men for beer and cigarettes?

In the dry cool of the cloakroom
he makes his quaint high-school move:
hand on my wrist, hard. Eyes closed.
What damn fools they don't mind being!

I left work
in good light

but halfway
it began

to thicken
like pudding.
Smoke pudding.

I drove slow
into clouds

with the wheels
off the ground

and when I
stopped the car

was lathered
like a horse
just run home.

I was so
sad. So sad,

I wish I
knew strange words

to say it,
a mourning

73

language. Lost,
I drove through

a cloud bank
so heavy

it crushed ev-
erything flat,

and I haven't
come out yet.

He was smiling, leaning,
when I shrugged on my coat.
Shadow steeped in shadow,
the whites of his eyes bright.

> My eyes close against him.
> Sometimes my real life is
> enough: Dishes. Pansies.
> Grape-skin holding back flesh.
> Arc of the bridge over
> the river. Fog tonight.
> Chip's rounded brown shoulder.
> Touching his rubber thigh,
> a handful of that warmth.
> Nan's moon smoothness: all for
> my blind fingers to touch.

> *Skin is all you need, Frank.*
> What makes a breast finer
> than a baby's shoulder?
> Why would you like to hold
> my hips and not a child's,
> turning, sharp, in your palm?
> *Warmth is what we need, Frank.*
> Anyone's living breath.
> I get it where I can.
> I choose my small kingdom.

This knight in his freedom—
"Cora," he said to me
hard, through angry teeth.
"Cora, you're wrong. There is
no choice. You have two hands.
Two legs. Take both. *Take both.*"

What an old
dull story:
TEMPTING THE GOOD WIFE
(WHO HAS HER REASONS)

I let him—
in the parking lot—
put his face
up against my face.
Only his straw cheek
on my neck.

He swallowed my mouth.

Fry. I am
a virgin again,
weak with shock
to feel under his
uniform that magic
worm turn stone.

We stood locked
till it turned again.

Rain-logged.
Tear-logged.

"A good thing it's warm,
we'd have a storm like '48."

This post-
card's washed

clean. Who was it from?
Did Frank write to say "Forget it"?

Or Fry
from his

side of the bed: "Dear
wife, dear Cora, how do you do

me this
cruel way?"

Mistress
J. Hoyt

swirls the permanent
black ink to say "Shame."

Avon
Lady

threatens, "Come, come,
it's time to buy a new blusher."

It's me.
Just me—

a piece of paper
waiting like a headstone:

What will there be in the end,
the very end,
to say?

Storm high.
Power's off.

Out on the road
a candle wanders
into the dark night's mouth.

When you begin to see them
there are more dark corners than light.

I could hide in one and not be missed
until the children wake. God protect me.

I am my neighbor's candle wavering down
the long hill, flaring, till the wind
        snaps off my head.

My children nuzzle me.
They pull me back to them.
They see like everyone
I drift. I come undone.

Their father calls their names
over my head. Fishing
with Chipper, puzzling Nan,
too slippery to catch.
They ride their bikes past me
over my head.
                    He casts
his children in a ring
to battle my children.
But none of them will win—
they'll hobble, bleed, and cry,
and lose us both trying.

Now I'm drifting to sleep
stalled in the front window.
Let them go, all of them
back over my head, back
over the road's dark crest,
glide off the edge of the world
so I can sleep it off:

my long tired motherhood,
my nights as Mrs. Fry
that must have come out of a bottle—
why else the occasional singing,
and all that idiot trust,
fooling with this stranger?

My father looks away from me.

I should have married a farmer.

If I am irresponsible
behind the steering wheel again
he'll take my keys or turn me in.

(Fry ought to do it but he won't.)

What Father knows about Oxford
stays with the plows in the garage
downtown. What I know about it
should hover in my own kitchen,
over the range, maybe, like smoke.
It should not get out the window
where all of Oxford is breathing.
Next time they're loading the sander
or grading a washed-out shoulder,
it should not come back to him in
the filthy mouths of his own men.

My father looks away from me.
Now that harsh smoke floats between us.
It will not stay in my kitchen.
It will not settle out with time.
Mother waves her hands at the smoke
she knows well. My father's loving
face is gray and spoiled.

I'm sorry.

He's moved on,
the way men do.
His clean uniform
hangs on the cloakroom pole
waiting to be filled again
by someone between moves.

(Instead of leaving
the women change
their hairdos.)

I'm sorry he's gone.
I didn't get
to say yes
or no.

The Boston bus
is always late.
I count on it.

Nan flips pages,
Chip sleeps, wakes. Nan
needs the bathroom.
"It's a closet,"
my skeptic says.
I pick her up
over the gaping
hole. She holds her
breath till her feet
touch solid ground.
A careful girl.
I only wish
care made a damn
bit of difference
in the field of
set traps that wait
to snarl her feet.

Touching some shoulders
and every seat,
Nan dances down
the rocking aisle.

Fry in Boston
forgot his wife.

I am Fry's wife
in Boston.

Now I know how to survive the city:
If you have come stark naked, you can dress
yourself in the kind indifference of crowds.
If you come tired, you can sleep with strangers.
Everything is possible, nothing is
possible. Go empty and come home full,
go full and come home empty. As you like.
Word will never seep over the state line
of what atrocities you have done here.

Park Street.   I cower behind my children.

The old witch thrusts one hand, to the elbow,
in the trash basket. It rocks
and steadies. One banana
black as a stick. A bottle
of vicious green soda turned to swamp scum.

My children point. They knead my hand and stare,
impolite. Can you see her
ready herself for bedtime,
pull her toes in through their holes,
wrap her killed nose in a sock for warming?

I'll bet she thinks she's Sheba lying back
in her coal bin. No one puffs
at her door, or in her ear.
She is how used and lonely
you can get. She makes Charity hide out

panicked, behind the Prudential Center.
Did the moon ever move her?
She hung such lovely laundry . . .
What a gathering of flies
inside her open coffin.
But they find she's all seamed up.

She makes me float and wander.
Keep me warm, children, keep me warm.
Need me.

Why do we need the Public Gardens—
this is Nan—
when we live in a Private Garden
of our own?

■

My caterpillar
Chip says, from the bench
he's hanging from:
Too many feet, Mom.
Now can we go home?

■

Mom looks at her hands.
Like her worn face, lined
with what is called "life"
by some optimists
who hunt down the deep
folds for "character."

Oh, the old joke—half
full? Half empty? Half
lived? Half died? Pale now
and ready to make
peace because peace is
where you can go barefoot
and empty-handed
without protection.
Anger, like Boston
(to quote my wise son),
has too many feet.
Let's go find some quiet.

In the fall dark
under no moon
the bus steals back
through closed-down towns.
Candia, Bow,
the mild hills of
sleeping Claremont.
Our driver pulls
quietly up
to the locked doors
of all the banks.
A cat burglar
would make more noise
twirling the locks
of jewel safes.
They gape like tombs
for a second
and then slam shut
without a sound.
What does he leave
in that briefcase?
Secrets, secrets,
money maybe,
maybe better:
potions, lovers'
vows, terrible
threats. What does he
take? We're his sack-
ful of sleepers
with smiles on our
faces, strangers
head to head. I

sit bolt upright
waiting for hope
to get past me,
confidently
to put its hands
inside my chest,
to slow my breathing
but let me live.

Fry takes
the sleeping babies
one by one
from me.

Tucked back
in their own blankets,
he kisses
their eyes.

I see
he walks stiffly
as though he's
been *still* . . .

And just
as well. Sat still
and worried,
swayed in the

tidal pull
that brought me home
and still could
drown us all.

I turn
to him. I reach
and just touch him.
Careful now.
I take him back.

Something
flares a second
and in its small light
I see our faces:
almost calm.

the first frost
my God   like
death you know
it's coming
but you mourn
you never
quite believed

iced leaves   limp
marigolds
smothered black
a battlefield
squash blossom
survivors
gold   grinning

this morning
I looked out
where winter
is waiting
in the field
white as a
Halloween
ghost   but real

the wheel turns faster
going down
with the year

Boots: in a box
under the bed.
I prop them like
rubber bookends.
Two clean snowsuits
hang on these pegs
till cold chases
the children quick
into their arms.
Fry takes hot lunch
in his thermos.

At five o'clock
he tracks snow paws
onto the rug.
But it's too warm—
they glow once, then
blink out like old stars.

CORA FRY'S

PILLOW BOOK

March and the ice is breaking up in the brook out back
below our house. It cracks like gunfire, a sudden
report, shocking and sharp. *How can this be water?*

Some days I hear it booming, deep
and slow, heavy as thunder. Then
the thin uncertain trickle starts. Spring,
that gentle birth—bells of blue hyacinth break through the snow,
birds through their crust of shell—is anything but gentle.

The earth's membranes tear. The flow thickens.
Each year I learn not to be sentimental: birth
is the death of another season.

They need a sign: **No mothers in the body shop!**
I call out "Chip!" and my voice is a dropped wrench, loud
as I can make it. In the dead light, motes swirling, standing still,
caught in its oil, black rags, sour iron smell, the hissing and clanging,
through it all I can barely make out his features. And he turns away in
    a rage.
I call out to him again but he is so ashamed of my softness here—
as if they are his fault, my breasts, I know it. My hips
in worn blue cotton. My hair that fuzzes at my neck inviting breakage.
Broken already.
Everything in here is harder than I am, the tools' thick surfaces, the
    machines, chuffing,
that eat the bolts off tires, the dangle
of fan belts cluttered on the wall behind him, and nozzles like parts of
    his body
I mustn't see anymore—he is embarrassed for himself, so reduced. Not
for me, this is:
for himself and the others. For Jimmy
back in the office and Horace out front pumping gas, gabbing. For baby Fitz
who just last week married his pregnant sweetheart and she's already
guilty as I am, swelling up in secret, scaring the boy half to death. When
    I talk to my son
he hits a button and a silver car rises
and rises between us on a hard oiled stalk.
He keeps to the other side of it, poking
its underparts. He is the only man in the shop, of course,
who came out of such a delicate darkness as mine. The only one
who cried when they lifted him up from his bloody nest, lunging and
    gasping. As if
he was born cold as a wrench or a hammer, slicked shiny with motor
    grease.
As if I was ever
as fragile as he thinks I am today.

I.

I'm listening, I said.
She never came by so early but this time she took the kids to school and
        turned around,
rushed over while the mist was still thick over the brook, just lifting
its long gray wing. Air still harsh on the skin with morning.
She took the road like she was being chased, pebbles flying, dust when
        she stopped, a geyser.
"Cora," she said, and she flung down in a chair (heavily, though she
        was not heavy),
her skinny self, her bag that said HOT STUFF in pink yarn roses,
her curls disheveled, herself a rose, over-ripe,
and asked for a shot of coffee. Head in her hands,
always dramatic. Doomed. "A shot!" I laughed. "How strong do you
        think I make it!"
"This isn't funny."
"I never said it was." But I was sorry.
I bit my lip and poured and sat. "Tara." Soft as I could. She smiled
like someone who could see a thousand miles into the distance
over Crane Mountain, halfway to Boston, but went there, searching,
        alone,
no one invited.

Such push-pull, talk-don't talk, and I sat with my hands
in my lap, obedient, while the coffee heated,
waiting to hear what she came for and
didn't we know it would come.

And when it came I couldn't think anything but Damn,
nobody gets through, then, without a blot or a smear—Reverend Slate
would sigh: weakness, common as mildew,
dark spots spreading everywhere, a contagion.

Damn: She couldn't *not*. He didn't want to *not*. Dink, his name was.
   Dink.
I should have guessed. So: She had Curly. He had someone named Jan.
   Children
galore, between the two of them. And Curly faithful,
God knows—Curly who's been stunned for years
that this woman seems to want him. (He thickens,
she thins. Why didn't I see it coming.)
She met him—Dink—at the office of the County Clerk. Such innocents.
Citizens, shoulder to shoulder.
Her neck was knotty when she cried.
They'd never spent the night, all of it stolen,
rushed, terrible, thrillingly wild,
Oh Cora, you can't imagine—and she was right, I couldn't. (Not
that I didn't try.) The pure pain of it. Savage, the tearing
when they left each other, as if they were parting for good,
for exile across the ocean. Her lovely face as ravaged
as ever I'd see it, raw and fragile,
frayed at the eye sockets, all worn. I didn't want details,
did, didn't. The way she wanted to tell me,
not tell me, tell me, a light
flashing on/off, on/off on the two of us
caught in it full, showing too much that we didn't
want seen. "He touches me," and her face was young as her youngest
   daughter's
in spite of the eyes,
"and I'd die, I'd give my life away, I swear, for a single finger
there." Imagining Fry, the idea of dying for any part of him,
let alone a finger.

The questions I swear I asked to make her feel better, not worse.
Trying to calm her, edge her over: Think of your girls, your boy,
    the dangers, real ones,
trading them in like this for a passing passion. "Oh,
I should have expected, you can't bear the thought of anyone
happy in bed!" I tried to soothe
the craziness out, like smoothing wrinkles from a sheet,
regular, slow. "Just *think*," I said. "It's you I care about, you
in a year, alone. Five years. Well and good, bed,
the esctasy part. Will he leave his wife for you?"
Think? "This isn't about shared bank accounts," she scolded me,
her face gone red, "shared names or shared beds," it was the way
they lit up the sky like a burning oil well. The howling,
animals finding each other after so long. Her curls collapsed, live petals
    suddenly drying, going brown.
Her breasts, I saw, at the top of her shirt
were on their way to long and stringy: this was the moment
before her life looked all too much like mine. No wonder
she had to tell me. She wept for my life that must seem to be coming
    at her, its mildew, its spreading blankness.
"Do you need my permission?" I asked her that.
(This is, I swear, where *All My Children* comes from, *As the World
Turns*, this is where it goes.) "What
are friends for?" she dared me back,
and handed me coffee cold in the mug. Hard,
harder than I'd ever seen her, thin-lipped, she talked to the door.
"Curly I love, Curly is *good*. But Dink—
he makes me real, he makes me a woman. No,
Cora, remember? Well, maybe you don't. That's what it is: A never-been-
    touched.
A girl."

She roared away, not comforted, I guess, but not dissuaded either,
to spend the morning mooning over the clothes in her dryer, the luncheon
    meat. *Howling?*
I tried to imagine
the animal that would make me bark
and startle. That could make me gamble my life
for a single moment of burning. Exile? Never-been-touched?
Never-been-touched? Then, honey,
I'm the girl.

II.

This wasn't, by a long shot, finished yet.
All of it hit
what they like to call the fan, the men do.

After she told Curly (to hurt him?—I don't know—
to get his blessing? Are women cruel
only to tender men, to the ones
who'll bleed?) the other names began to float to the top
like bodies carelessly buried: Rod Smythe over to Dalton.
That new cop, the redhead? Everywhere I turn I see
my friend now, bare in somebody's headlights,
some pickup, some diesel cab, some narrow
trailer bedroom. The minister's assistant, that summer boy
who looked lickspittle clean, I hear
(though I don't have to believe) tried to kill her with his bare hands (not
    so clean
as we thought) when she tossed him out
like a tissue she found in her jacket pocket.

That morning in my kitchen,
the virgin overwhelmed,
she kept the hard part in,
let the easy out.
For what?

Is a friend
only your mirror?
A still pond you lean down over (the White Rock goddess!)
to see who you want to see?

I know she needed something—comforting—but not
from Cora. No—my friend no more my friend, gone somewhere I can't
    follow—
not from *me*.

The Carroll Stitts are moving. "Moving,
Cora!" Impossible! They have the brook, my mother says,
bent at the waist with hard feelings. They have a view
of the mountain, unobstructed, those luscious
acres, three daughters salted around town, with kids
and a dozen in-laws, and a road
with their name on it. A trailer for their son
who's saving to build, and their youngest, Tina,
Employee of the Month at the drive-in bank.

"Why?" she asks the way you ask
about a murder or a suicide. "Don't we have everything
here?" We do, Ma,
we surely do. It seems they want the city. They want
some dazzle, she tells me. They've seen the ads
and bought the package: the rink at the mall
that's never snowed over. The high rise with the elevator, the balcony.

A balcony! she snorts, as if it's a Rolls-Royce and who would want one.
Her back porch, like mine, hangs over a greening garden,
the brook, the inquiring
ducks. What does a balcony look out on
but a river full of traffic—rubbish floating downstream—and guns
no hunter'd recognize. Her friends
go to the Stitts' "Yard Sale of a Lifetime,"
bring home canning jars, sap buckets, the old sturdy kind
still sweet in the grain, decoys, drills. My mother
boycotts the day. She knows betrayal,
she knows surrender, those Christians turning pagan on her.

She knows insult. And asks me, shyly, if I'm tempted.
"Ma! By what?" I'm shocked. You only get one home

in this lifetime, and this one's mine, as if she didn't know it.
She only wants to hear the words, like a vow. Bred in my flesh,
I tell her. Like a fingerprint. A watermark,
the shadow of all those lives before me,
Hubberd and Fry, in the graveyard now.

The only time I had to see New York,
remember? On the way to that wedding in Virginia? We planned it—
Fry did—so we could pass it at night
the way they say you should cross Death Valley: with a water bag,
gas in the tank, food for emergencies, and the promise
not to stop, no matter what
comes to the window.

I used to stroke my strong brown calves
as if they were wood I had to keep buffed
to a high shine. My arm was wicked,
I'd single out a sapling across the garden and nail it
with an apple. I had a good eye,
believe me, and the will they love to talk about: what
heart.

But I was the pitcher's little sister, the ball girl—they gave me that
as a sop—to shut me up. I had to watch,
hungry. My favorite part was the ballet
when someone's feet came up, up off the grass
on a high fly, or when he flung himself flat out, arms splayed like a
        diver's,
at the plate—that split second before
choice, when winning was better
than living. Could I have done it if they'd let me? If they hadn't laughed,
hitching and spitting and scratching, lewd as monkeys in the zoo.

I can't say I hate my husband, my brother,
and the boys downtown (their bellies over their belts now,
hair growing wild as ryegrass out of their ears) but I haven't forgiven them
either, their thousand innocent noxious little ways, how
(brother or no brother) they will never learn
I'm no one's little sister.

The fight flares up fast, like a barbecue catching.
Back near the cars where the ground's already scuffled
Tim and Maxwell, fists up, circle and feint,
looking for a face to wash in the hot bare dirt.

Somebody tells me they work side by side, eat
lunch together—they need the company picnic once a year
to clear the air, heavy between them these days
(though words, like tools, could fix it if they dared)

or is it only too much beer?
There's always a fight, the same old ruckus:
Men turn into jeering boys, playground bullies,
playground goats. Their wives are not impressed.

I watch Tim's son when his father hits
the dust, the little flare of envy in his eyes,
even for loss. Don't learn this lesson, I'm thinking. His mother
covers her face. Tim's up again, charging. What can she offer

but a plea: Be careful dodging the cars in the meadow!
Don't climb the fences! She teaches the boy to say hello
like a gentleman. Here's Kool-Aid in a paper cup (say thank you),
an introduction to someone's geeky daughter

who smiles, a smear of mustard in her braces.
One word raised against their damn-fool dads
will finish us with these sons. I lie back out of it, cover my face with my
        hat
and dream of China, where I've heard they eat
live birds right in the shell like a four-minute egg, and love it.

The way they tell it: how they used to
find her, Joanie, hiding in all the improbable places—
under the couch like a new kitten, inside
the freezer, but it was old and didn't close tight enough
for damage. She was only cold
when they pulled her out, dewed with frost
like her own lawn in October: Unhurt
beyond the hurt she dragged in with her. Imagine
lying down in your coffin, pulling the top down on your grief, watching
the little light go out,
as if you were meat.

Pretty soon they could predict
where she might have gone this time—a joke. How cruel
for your pain to make you a habit, a chore,
a laughingstock. Nobody blamed them, her husband, her children, fellow
	sufferers,
but anyway how cruel. And she'd have heard it all.

So when the fire truck, Dickie Shaw bent over the wheel,
gunned up the road and clamored across the bridge and turned her corner
I closed my eyes and hoped for the best and knew,
but couldn't dream her dream.
She didn't want us to.

Gasoline in the bathtub (the drain pulled shut), in a ghastly circle,
splashed against the door and the door bolted,
key heaved out the window.
No snow, down to the sod, from the heat,
and there was the key glittering like a jewel the next morning.

I was dry-eyed when I heard—
horror, anger/ relief maybe: that she got
exactly what she wanted. There's all kinds of wanting.
She was always good,
God, I remember this now, at the crafty things—
cakes in the shape of fairy godmothers, a castle
of Popsicle sticks for the day-care sale,
découpage and macramé—all those French-named hobbies—
and valentines you could disappear in, gobs of doily-lace, whipped
      cream, and then
eat. Smiley faces. The Queen of Do-It-Yourself (is this grim?)
did it herself.

I think she wanted to be, at the end, only invisible.
When they came searching this one last time
they wouldn't find her, only a trail of ash,
and her house gone too, the handmade lampshades, the sweet
      dust ruffles.
Nothing left of the world except a narrow strip of fury
on which, satisfied,
she struck the match.

Yes, his head leaves that deep dent in the pillow,
that grayish slope. Sleeping,
he trusts me simply, the way his hound does, Trapper,
flung like a rug at his feet.

Home at the dark end of the day
he wants his dinner, his channel, and a glass of silence,
and he doesn't want to
have to ask.
His eyes are red from working,
worn, heavy, just beyond
soothing. Once I'd have kissed them closed.

Does he miss that time, I wonder, his shy eyes
with those lush lashes, womanish almost,
I loved so much? Those smart hands, no belly,
no droop, no dewlaps?

Does he remember me
across this trench time's gouged in the kitchen, me
here, stacking dishes, sweeping up crumbs?
No matter how little we eat, the crumbs
will fall, the way sleep gathers in the corners of your eyes
whether you sleep or not.

I.

The night my cousin Fran sits weeping
that God has closed her womb—even so she lives on the Bible,
its thick rich words flooding her veins like blood,
and her pronouncements monumental—I'm chained
between the telephone and the window, waiting for a voice or a face
as if God might show himself there: my only son

is off again with the same dumb
daredevil deadbeat do-nothing boys
who have nothing to lose but their licenses or their lives. Not one thing
I know about them soothes me. Fry
thinks he's helping, laughing it off, reminding me how his mother
wrung her hands just so, and wept.
Called the police: "Arrest those boys
if you catch them with a bottle."

Three a.m., Fran long gone home, Chip stumbles in
and the ivy wilts, I swear, over the sink,
at the smell of him. Behind the bedroom door, breathing again, I'm free
to ask of God, Which of us is luckier, Fran
in her barrenness, who doesn't have to wait
for a face under the porch light
(her son's or the chief of police with bloody news),
or me, who can barely remember the infancy
Fran never dreams beyond—white lacy pillow in the pram,
sweet smell of the top of the sleeping baby's head—or even the
        pregnancy,
the shower of delicate promises, the simple waiting
she thinks is everything?

II.

There was once another of us at the table. What
does my mother see when we sit now
shoulder to shoulder, Sam and me?

Sam remembers her, he says, but
only by the littlest things: how red and blue barrettes,
like gumballs, held her hair. The smell of her talcum
after the baths they took together. He doesn't know
what she was *like*, he says—she was too young
to be like anything.

Her name was Lacy, after a family of Irish
somewhere back on the tree. I always thought that was lacy,
like-a-doily, I'd picture her baby hands
in the holey, hand-shaped maple leaves flung down on the lawn.
eaten to the bare ribs. I'd lift a handful and look
through a tender crumbling leaf to nothing
on the other side. By then I knew
that's what she was: some strange and whispered nothing, and I—
had I come to take her place? But *I* was *me*.
It made no sense.

Mother didn't talk about her much, but I could see
her eyes fill sometimes, for no visible
reason. My mother had a mystery life I was jealous of,
a grief so large my being here could never replace it. Gone,
I learned well, and quick, and early,
was better than Right Here, spilling things,
disobeying, fighting with Sam until we got the palm
of our father's hand: Lacy, before she had words to object,

was delivered into perfection, a heavenly consolation
for not being real anymore, and every year
I grew past her baby picture (mouth like a Cheerio, a fountain of hair
    gushing
up through her head) I thought: Doomed. But I meant myself.
There was no glamour in it, living. Dead,
she stopped while she was still ahead, that innocent
favorite, I thought, which did me harm
while it did her—poor lacier than thou—
no earthly good.

My children won't remember me the way
I see my parents: Up on the barn roof years ago
on her seventieth birthday, my mother shoveling snow—
thick clouds of it drifting down like the whole sky moving—

and my father receiving them, ducking, laughing,
smoothing the blue-white, stony shoulders
of the hugest snowman I've ever seen.

In my memory their cheeks are always red with effort, their mouths closed
(true or not) against complaint.

When it wasn't snow, I think it was haying time—high hay forever,
and rain approaching. Neither dared under-
estimate the other: Would the work get done
if they stopped believing? Neither slept much.

The energy my mother stirred up sweeping
would run my household on FAST FORWARD for a week.
We've lost, I think, some last turn of the mainspring. I don't know why

but Fry's got softer shoulders than the snowman at full melt,
and I'm afraid of heights.

Thelma was the one in our class most likely to—
we didn't know what, but we *knew*. She scared the boys
because she had a voice like an organ note,
loud and long and thicker than other voices,
and she never forgot a fact or remembered
an insult, never backed off, made herself
useful three places at once. Imagine
how the teachers loved her and didn't hide it. She was so alive you couldn't
dislike her, though it was terrible how many did.

They used to call her Never-Been-Kissed and
worse, and the girls were hardly better: she wasn't much
of a girl to them. What Thelma was made for was
leaving Oxford and never looking back, her shoulder
fitted to the wind like something Chip calls
aerodynamic.
                    But here she is,
arrived on time for class reunion with a brood as large
as anyone's—twin beauties under a shifting cloak
of starlet hair, a boy long-legged, sweet
and confident, whose teachers probably love him too. "The law's
absorbed my energies" is how she answers
questions, which makes folks gape. Her tweedy husband
keeps his hands in his pockets and hugs the doorway
close to the exit.

There's whispering over the finger foods.
"I always thought she was—*you* know,"
says Dickie Wells, who was voted cutest. "She *talked*
so much. And none of us could ever impress her." Well, then.
People are shy in her shadow. They go out to look

at her car that's the color of good whiskey
aged in the barrel. It has a letter
on the back that shows they bought it
somewhere in Europe. Imagine the bumper sticker:
THIS CAR HAS CLIMBED THE ALPS!

But she isn't there to gloat. Thelma wouldn't—I was
her friend for good reason. She walks from cluster
to cluster asking questions, smiling
like someone who means it. She tells her children
who starred in the Senior Follies, remembers
the basket Toby Simmons made that won a big one (though she says
she remembers him much taller). She doesn't do a thing
to make us feel jealous or left behind and that's what's hard
to take, I guess: to some it's worse
than gloating. It's holier than we are, because we couldn't be half
so nice ourselves. Dickie says, sly, "I bet it's politics
she learned that from. I bet she runs for office
down there wherever it is she lives. I be damned if I'd forgive
the things we did to her."

                Sunday I ask my minister
to speak sometime on Charity Rebuffed. People are funny,
he tells me, not amused—the generous ones
keep on paying sometimes. No matter what, he says
(already hunting, I see in his eyes, for a Bible verse to pin it to),
we keep them in debt forever.

When my mother took to her bed,
her face gone soft as a tea towel,
her voice the narrowest fraying thread, we stood
and wept and prayed and fretted
that she not turn mortal on us,
she who had been invincible, as hard
and fast, as steady-burning, as ironwood.

But this was only practice,
a rehearsal for the real—at dawn
there she was at her breadboard, singing.
Was the spell for her only, to introduce
her slowly, a glimpse, to the mere idea of weakness?
Or was the brush of that shadow-wing
meant for the rest of us, so damnably helpless,

that angel springing open the coffin door
just long enough for a wind to cross her kitchen
and keep the bread from rising?

Gardenia skin /
Nan's skin—her shoulder
fine-veined, tender, strong,
but yet so delicate the boy who pins the flower on,
piercing her dress with a long pearl-handled dagger,
stares awed and clumsy, like a new father
touching his baby's bottom for the first time with his callused hands.

I guess we've made it through. How my daughter's life
spins on into the future now
without me! I've handed her over (to walk on her own two feet)
into the world's wide arms.
Do you know what worry runs under
the bumpy surface of motherhood like a hidden brook, cold
and clear and continuous? What terror we won't *last* to see
this childhood through to some private, unsayable
Independence Day?

Would an animal feel shame the way I would have, to be ankle-seized,
up-ended, while her cubs—her foxes—sleep in the lair, innocent,
about to starve without her? Would she imagine their tails,
their bushy, lush, improbable red tails wrapped full around each other
for warmth, for comfort? And as she is murmuring to them "Oh
        wait for me!"
furious and hungry, quaking with cold, they begin to practice
forgetting her.

Nan holds my hand until we come to the heavy
dorm door, push it open, prop it patiently
for the others coming up behind.
They check each other out

like babies in their strollers who always knew
their own, focused and stared,
amazed they'd found another
so like themselves.

We carry our children's bags
and put them down where we're told to.
A few bold mothers bristle with hints
from a lifetime of decorating crises,

but they're ignored discreetly. Furniture trades places all around us.
A minute-and-a-half and the balance has subtly shifted:
We may pay the bills but
this is their home. We are their visitors.

Only when we leave—Nan is stacking
her sweaters into leaning towers of color,
talking over her shoulder, not to me—
their real lives will begin

and mine, my darling daughter,
with a stroke fainter and slower than any crow's-feet,
start to end.

In my dream I was in a place that had no weather.
It was what you imagine after the bomb: the grass
no-color, no smell in the air and the sky gone blind.

In the dream I went poking around in cupboards, under hedges,
searching for snow, or sun, or what I suddenly needed
more than another breath—rain, long fingers, wet and cool,

to stroke my head. But it was all transparent,
and against the fence where my zinnias grow, and the sweet purple
     alyssum,
were the heads of children, eyeless, on long waxy stalks

like poison shepherd's crooks that grow in the woods,
like the smudged-out stare of fetuses, those buds,
before they feel the print of their promised faces.

I thought it would be just
a jolly job: work that demanded doing,
out in the light, the sun, the morning
cracking open bright as a fresh-hatched egg,
and no one to keep tabs on me
but the sight of my neighbors eyeing their raised red flag,
waiting. Or the others who forget to wait,
surprised at what shows up with their name on it.
(Jim Cartwright has a boxful of naked breasts. Dixie Teal,
whale-shaped or not, dreams of models built like ten-year-olds.
Catalogs come, grandeur we can't afford,
so on, so forth, so unpredictable.) The mail arrives,
of course it arrives, a rhythm,
something to depend on,
a voice (I call it)—a voice for the eyes.

I heft the gray sacks, limp, shifting
like bodies, all corners, edges.
They're fierce, bottled up in there,
the points and angles of dozens of envelopes
sharper than dog teeth.
I never gave it a thought—inside the envelopes the *words*
must be the dogs themselves, some quiet,
some howling. My first day, up on the County Road,
a young man I didn't know grabbed his packet of letters out of my hands
and cursed before he even read a thing. Then
he threw a stone, hard, that cratered my bumper
and made me veer into the incoming lane.

It's only the ones I catch in a state
of longing who confess:

Eleanor Clymer's waiting
for her daughter to write forgiveness.
A red heart on the envelope, maybe,
or just a dumb word: "How are you? I am
fine." She's in a Halfway House in Texas
(San Antonio? Amarillo? Something,
she says, with an "a" in it). "I offended her,"
she tells me, looking unconvinced. (Eleanor can offend,
believe me, even if you're not
her daughter.) I remember Sandy—a tiny thing with curls,
who grew into an "uncontrollable,"
leaning on drugs, on men, on
"sissy crime," outside her mother's line of vision
but not (apparently) the law's.

Every day, she complains, I put a great big
nothing in the mailbox.
Today the box is bursting but look—no hearts, no greetings: no
thanks. At the end of my route, passing, I see
Eleanor, like her or not, dragging back to the house in her
floppy mules, bent and listing like someone with a bad
stitch in her side.

That girl—what power she wields,
fierce as a voodoo curse, just
turning her head away!

And Nathan Bing—he looked
like he was killing time when I drove up,
fussing with his periwinkle border. I could see
a talker on my hands. (That's fine unless I'm late.
And I was late.) "Did you know, Cora,"
he said in his raspy whisper, "I've got a little
ol' gal down in Belize."
And the "leeeze" seemed to take
forever. Out of his shabby jacket pocket
he flips a photo: Grinning, a dark young woman
under a halo of braids—I think his daughter's older—
with teeth the color of Nathan's edging stones,
white as a cuttlebone. She looked eager enough
to please. They hadn't met
yet—"We get on fine by mail"—but he wanted to bring her up here
before the winter came on to shock her.

Nathan's wife died slowly a long time ago,
after she wore him down to a nub.
His eyes are still tired, his shoulders a little
dogged, but I liked the cheer of his good intentions.
"Don't she look like a live one? And they speak English,
you know, so they're all ready. These letters she sends—"
He leaned in to keep a secret. "One time
she sent me a butterfly. Dead, of course. But she said
it was her spirit. A beautiful blue
with spots. These spots on the wings, like eyes.
That's not your everyday
kind of woman who'd do that, you know." And he shook
that day's letter at me. It rattled.
"Sounds like seeds—pumpkin,

flower—she sends me the oddest things."
He looked moonstruck as any boy,
standing with his feet in the green-black leaves of his periwinkle,
their shy star-flowers shining over the tops of his shoes.

I always envied Lucy McCarthy's—
the house, not the woman, I mean. That tall
brick double-chimney, angled toward the road,
1794 over the front door. Noble.
Whoever built that beauty had power my father never dreamed of;
I'll bet he lies in the graveyard flanked by wives.

My mother remembers Lucy beautiful too: blond and cool,
the kind who barely saw a soul around her, noble
in the way of houses and women who cast shadows
across the rest of us. She came back after a life invisible
to Oxford: home, to some, is only a house to die in,
in the end. Could that be all?
Home just a roof and a chair, a narrow bed
and a dim light in an endless hall?

Now, you see, you don't just bring the mail to Lucy McCarthy's.
You brake the car in the long drive under the sumptuous
maples, you tiptoe up the broken stone step—tap
at the door—enter—call.
I guess you'd call it a mercy, this daily ritual.
And like a queen in a rotted throne, Lucy, alone
the way she wants it, sits in the dark in the middle of a story:

How she danced, too tall for heels, in the flimsiest little
shoes, how she dined with kings I've never heard of, and met
the President on the way to the rest room
in Kenosha, Wisconsin, she doesn't say how (which makes me
wonder). Her baby's ears went bad when a seizure took him
but later he played first base (or was it first *bass*? She forgets to say
if it's music or baseball) with his arm in a sling, and married
the boss's daughter who hated him but went on loving

her. She's loved,
she's hated. When she broke her hip nobody visited.
She wrote down all the names of the ones who didn't remember
to come, but they'll remember what they forgot, she says,
the day her will is read.

I don't have time for the soaps anymore
but I have Lucy, no longer noble
under her brittle crown of braids.
Like a tap that can't be closed, the flow
of her memory floods the rooms no worse than Sam-
loves-Annie-who's-being-stalked-by-Jim-
whose-money-is-Leslie's-but-Leslie's-dying-
saved-by-a-doctor-whose-wife-is-suicidal.
Pause for commercial.

Lucy inventing, rearranging—the plot is fluid, as if she's watering down
the dust with her endless flow. A clouded dignity
clings to the old wood, the shadowy stenciling,
the cavernous fireplace, rooms where life throbbed up two centuries ago
like a fire leaping with light. The house, I suppose,
has outlived stronger women.
                            When I say my goodbyes
and close the heavy door, gently, and flee the smell of cats,
that moldy ammoniac edge, she's attending a debutante party
with Prince Radziwill, who was somehow involved with the Kennedys
later, much later, and her gown was one-of-a-kind,
off-the-shoulder, shocking, and her hair the same,
swept to the side like Veronica Lake's, but blond. She looks
as happy as anyone not fifteen minutes home from the ball,
and who's to say she's not? She quivers with pleasure.

I have put her mail in her lap unopened:
The catalog whispers to her, cruelly, Victoria's Secret.
She's won the Publisher's Clearing House jackpot
like the rest of us, which could help with these bills if it were only
true. When I come calling the next noon,
Lucy's lap is empty
and we start again.

Me buttoned into my flannel,
stretched out on a sheet of cotton candy-stripes
I've bought and washed, bleached, folded, stacked—

Marlene, Marilyn, Madonna, none of the silky sultry heroines
ever whispered, "Time to buy a new mattress, darling,
this one's gone soggy," or chased the dog off the quilt

when he's left, like a spray of pine needles after a storm,
half his spiny coat. The three delicious M's make the bed
ride soft as a boat on water. No one but a wife

worries if the springs are shot.
I know he feels it too, Fry does. He must. Thermal tights and baggy
boxer shorts heaped on the chair together—less than he hoped,

back when even a boy is a dreamer. Enough
or not enough? That, like the nap on corduroy,
seems to depend on the light. His thick back's sturdy, a tree stump

against my own, and mine is—I can't imagine. Ask him.
So many years of breathing in ragged
unison. Drifting away on a sentence. Rolling together

in that soft, deep runnel down the center of the bed.
When the thunder's bad, we still stay up like kids, singing.
I heard him laugh once in his sleep.

Is this what the light years bring?

It seemed to fall more than once a year,
the Labor Day Parade. I rode my father's iron shoulders
while, proud as a boy with his first car, he rode
the centerline in his farting '33 Bearcat,
its furious goose of a horn squawking, its flanks
shiny as well water.

I'd wave like a princess or a general
coming home from war triumphant.
Conquering heroes big and small, and the town spellbound
by a tradition fixed as a holy ritual,
we shared the dumb conceit—I only see it now—
of those who have done nothing
but who own something.

Which would he choose,
if the choice were only his:

to look the wreck of my strong-shouldered,
rasp-skinned, whiskery, grater-voiced
father—bones like a rack
of antlers, with a moose's vigor—
who pinched me hard and tore
the cartilage from sentiment
and spat it out, grizzle and soft gut,
for the dog to do away with in his corner?

Or this velvet-skinned, whispery
quiverer, a few frail fronds of hair
pulled sheepishly across his skull, his fingers
sharpened to pincers reaching for something
sweet, and dropping it?
I can't identify this man who gums the air
for words, except for a slight familiar
slant of brow, a turn or two of phrase
that strikes some echo—a curse
when he drops the cookie—but nothing
sure, no trusty recognition.

My father was never like that, I'd say
if you asked me. My fierce father—
that ice-cold splash of beer-in-the-face,
that bite, that bark-and-a-laugh,
that quick embarrassed hug—
hasn't been here for a couple of years.
To tell you the honest truth I don't know
where he is.

My mother didn't talk much.
She worked around us, sopping the table clean
between our elbows, vacuuming
under our feet. We ran
from one room to another to escape
her quiet eye.

But there wasn't anything she didn't know
that she needed to. This was how they did it
then: whatever sin
we'd been caught in, no judge,
no jury, we went straight
as returning felons to our sentencing.

She'd bring it to Father
like a cat with a gift-bird in its mouth
and tenderly lay it beside the kitchen door.
If it isn't dead,
she meant (too kind to find a way
herself), you kill it. And

"for your own good, with love," she always said,
he would.

I forget it's strange how fog seeps out of the river
every day till the weather turns.

How, each warm morning, blinded drivers inch down the road
on faith alone. The bright eye of the school bus pokes a hole
in the muzzy air, and then drives slowly through it.

In the river valley, something invisible is always
coming toward you. Every stop sign, every hunkering truck

blooms out of nowhere, much too close
when you finally see it. One day it's going to cost me my life,
creeping this slug-trail, getting the mail out blind.

I never knew how odd it was until
I spent my first night far from the river.

Then I learned that summer morning is born in light,
most places. The air had cleared its throat and its voice
was pure: sunlight, sharp outlines, deep shadows.

What we, when the fog burns off,
call afternoon.

Saturday: Every steel bolt in the store,
every pull chain, wing nut, U-shaped crotch of pipe,
socket wrench, glass cutter, newfangled glue
calls to him the way birds speak
to birders in the wild.

Coming home, I watch him point the way
for a driver lost at the stop sign, how his limber hands
move precisely, like a bandleader
shaping the music, the stops, the flow of the trip.
He promises a grand finale.

And now, as twilight begins to tighten
around the garden like a giant net, he props
the last pear tree in its hole. He kneels,
one pantsknee in the muck, one clean—always the same one clean—
heaping dirt around its base, soothing as water.

Enthusiasm moves him, pulls him through his day,
roughly. His chores are games to win
or lose. Busy, Fry's younger than his son,
for sure. More boyish with the years.

Think with your hands, feel, touch with your eyes, you get to watch
the whole solid world come to your knee,
and bend and calmly sit. I think I miss the pith, the core, the flesh.
    I think
I think too much.

Not the inches around my waist,
no longer invisible under the right kind of pleats.
Not the way I improve my hair with this magic
potion. (*Always test before using. Do not use on brows.*
Just leave them to their fate,
those little stabs of silver you can't tweeze out.)

Not weariness or cramping thumbs,
or the doctor who used to say casually "At your age . . ." and dismiss
me, and now says darkly "At *your* age . . ." and orders tests.
It's joy. It's promises kept, not broken.
Joy. I know you don't believe me.

It's every happy milestone that looms
and passes: Chip brings home Michelle,
freckled and sweet, and, watching them together,
I face the truth still shocked, under my welcoming smile, my wedding
hairdo, that the woman in his life is not
his mother.

Nan brings home from school
no man but a passion for rocks: Who would try
to daunt her? She doesn't climb them, she
collects them in a sack, carries it lightly, my light-limbed daughter,
as if it were filled with mushrooms, learns mouth-breaking names
I can't pronounce, and now she's off
to a deep ravine in Arizona to pin
some weighty mystery down. I think
I envy her—not the gray basalt in a jagged hunk,
only the passion, the freedom to
care, to go, for its own sweet sake.
"*Relationships* aren't everything," she says,

and I can see by the way she rolls her eyes
what she thinks of me.

But I said it was the milestones: how each time
something happens that we have always expected—
events tolling like bells, never quite surprising—
what can I think of but the final
stone to come, the day they tell us will also arrive,
sooner, later, but no way not arrive? They haven't lied
yet—we'd better believe them.

Each good day says This is what it is to live.
As you are now, so once was I.
Die, says the wedding day, *Die*, says the live birth.
Prepare yourself and follow me. And I do, I do,
now more than ever, every year, prepare.
A promise is a promise, it's only fair.
We raise a toast—"To Chip and Michelle then, cheers!"
The aftertaste of this sweet champagne is bitter.
No one would guess I know that,
seeing me smiling here.

Our families, Fry's and mine, are twined
by now like vines on a fence.
A hundred generations behind us, who
knows how many ahead,
and all of it balanced on the narrowest whim
we shared as hopeful children saying yes.
He took me—simple—I took him.

I got Fry's mother's picky eye,
the way she cruises my house for dust devils and hair balls
and shows them off like prizes—but then
she'll bring me her favorite rose geranium cuttings in water,
and plant them for me, cooing and soothing
as if they were her babies. He took my dad, his lofty
sense of himself, who kept the road and snowplows
as tenderly as some men groom their horses,
and stayed too long at the truck barn for Mother's pleasure.

Both of us inherited blowsy aunts
and blowhard uncles and dear ones, and each
one cousin out-to-lunch—one, minimum. And, among many, I got Fry's
        shy
sister Daisy I love so much, and he got Sam
he doesn't love an inch.

Pieces of fractured families fly around our heads like shrapnel
these days. It must feel like an accident
to the body—grandparents dismissed, like limbs
blown off! In Oxford, tiny battleground, eyes averted,
friendships torn up like expired contracts—
one branch of the family tree withers
in bitterness, leaving (uncancelable) its genes behind.

Take a long look at the strangers
you're going to bed with, Chip and Michelle.
You've heard it said but, children, it's truer than love—
you marry them all.

I.

There seems to be a shadow. They want another
look. Can a shadow
eat you up?

Ultra-sound: a perfect name
for the best in stereo—the living end.
But we look more than we listen.

I lie flat, as if I've fallen.
They slather my breast with jelly
the way I've buttered a lifetime
of sandwiches. Then they move
the little mouse—up, down, around,
grazing back, forward,
the ripples just like water
opening to let the nubbin shadow through, then sealing
over, and up it bobs again, and under. Gone.

I think of the beaver who lives in our brook—
the way he surfaces
and hides and comes up somewhere you never dreamed
of looking. I want to shout

"Well, are you *real?*"
This shadow's more like a thought
than a reality. Even the thought can't hold steady as fear can,
as pain. As amputation. Un-solid, un-
dangerous. Un-serious. It will have to get my attention,
I tell it, if it wants to

kill me. No.
Bravado.
It can kill me if it wants to
any way at all.

II.

For now
it won't. Somebody else
today. Behind my back
or yours, the headless, heartless,
mindless knot—worse than malicious
or angry or spiteful, less willful even
than a thundercloud—
is nothing.
Wants nothing.

Isn't even
laughing.

I.

Fry calls them *the ladies.*
I don't think it's funny.

The short-haired one is curt; all business,
she wears a tool belt, has a card: CONSTRUCTION, RENOVATIONS.
The long-haired one, red-cheeked as an apple,
likes to smile, and when I see her I smile back.
Fry frowns and looks insulted.

I've had to think it out but it isn't hard if you look and listen:
Theirs seems just about the way of every household:
the virtues alternate, the tempers, the natural inclinations.

II.

Nan has questions, though: How
can they love each other? Right
and wrong, that isn't it, but *how*.
Mechanics, she doesn't whisper, but clearly means. And whether the
    love
of someone like yourself is—
hard enough? Real? The awful challenge
she finds in the love of boys? There just might be comfort
in letting those characters get lost—she laughs—
the guys with the *hands*,
taking up all the space, making the noise.
The moves.
                I see how the future's still open
for her. Her whole life, I think, is like the fontanel, that soft spot
at the front of her infant head, before the plates of bone moved together
and closed. How, when she was still so soft,
anything could happen, could press itself into her for good, for bad,
maybe forever.

I.

So Fry—surprise!—has overheard my dreams.
For thirty years of here and now together,
he hands me this little gift he cannot lift or carry.

California!
Whenever I had trouble falling asleep
I'd drowse over my magazine and imagine

the electric blue shore tucking in, belling out—
humped rocks over the water, cliffs beetling down, bare,
on the chute of the coastal highway.

Our dark New Hampshire lakes reflect
the same old sky, dense woods,
tangled, familiar, doubled on the still surface.

How trapped we are in our inland here, how strange it will be
to lie down again after the touch of such a blue,
tight between these mountains.

II.

Who'd have guessed the Windex-colored water
is to be seen but not touched? The houses
are such colors as someone from home might dream

after too much Thanksgiving dinner, pink, yellow,
sunstruck dreams, and a rusty tile common as shingle.
Armored palm trees guard the cold white flash of facades,

mannequins shimmer under watery glass
that blurs (a mercy) the price tags at their feet.
LAX? Lax is the word—it was another country.

And I spent too much time thinking Oh,
how the children would have loved this! And Oh,
to have come when they were small! Live life

too long for others, when you're finally there—do you know the story
of the blind man cured, who got his sight
too late? He didn't know what to do with his eyes

but, weary, ask the doctor to blind him again.
I'll have to take the world
in baby steps, I think, and let my children bring me their stories.

How good, after all that light,
to be back in this huddle of green, in my soggy bed,
my cluttered, wood-faced kitchen.

How sweet to see
my moon hung on its old hook in the trees.

Dogs dream,
Fry tells me. Trapper lies,
a square knot coming loose, all curves
tucked over curves,
the fire-gleam bursting and falling
on her breathing side.

Dogs dream,
he says. My shelty, once—
this was before you knew me—the day a truck
took all her wind and tossed her up like a buckwheat pancake,
later I watched her sleeping and oh, she dreamed.

He shakes his head. Her feet jiggled
and spasmed, she panted like somebody scared to death. She must have
    dreamed
flying, I think. Falling. Breaking into a million feathers
floating off downwind where it didn't hurt.

What would glory be
behind those rutted lids? Deer like a blood fountain
and no one whooping, hot on her trail?
New road spooling out ahead, she never stops
and her nails don't click on the soft pine-
needle floor?

Trapper is running her gun-gray tongue
over her lips like a connoisseur. Invisible rumblings
shake her paunch. A shudder under the skin.
Ears up. Ears down.
Then suddenly like something dead—shot
in its tracks—a perfect silence. Scares me every time, the way
she gives herself to stone.

She wouldn't let him go. When my father died,
my mother clawed at the sheer sides of the cave
his life had long become, struggling for a handhold.

He didn't—he unclenched his fingers and let it slip away.
He didn't know her to the eye, though maybe
by some grudging hidden grace he did.

She tried to breathe for him. Bloodied,
she forgot her promise to see him to the end,
kiss him goodbye and step aside.

Is that why she seems more angry now than sad?
She begged him to wait for her
but he wouldn't wait.

Inside this pearl of snow
the light's so strong
and, underfoot,
the ground's sifted so smooth,

everything's one thing—
road, grass, the tops of the bushes,
the spindles of hearty weeds—
all slicked down white as if by the back of a spoon.

We're caught inside a paperweight. If
someone picked it up and shook it hard,
all of Oxford would float down slow
as the feathered sky, and settle rearranged:

wives in the wrong houses, children in the trees,
husbands in kitchens,
animals searching for masters who knew
their names, finding only strangers.

A hush, a hum of breathing,
and the snow flying up from the ground—
Maybe there'll be no Armageddon,
friends. Maybe this is the way, swaddled
and cold and silent, the world ends.

When I was a child, I hated
my brother the way you were supposed to,
to cover up the real story, envy
(though not of the extra part
they say we want: that silly spout,
always, I thought, in danger of accident,
a bad frost that could snap it off
like an icicle). I was only jealous of the Sam
who could twist my arm,
whose voice I could hear
through any door, any argument.
I was jealous of the fist
he didn't have to use.

I never thought we'd stop the angry tussle,
the wronged shout, the elbowing, the play for our parents' eye.
I never thought spouses and children, work, a dozen other choices,
would douse the sparks between us and make us kissing cousins.

I never believed we'd go home at the end of the day
to separate houses.

The hymns are a gentle hand
on my brow, I don't doubt it or regret it.
Of course I ask if it's God I love
in this pure white wooden place

(orderly rows, a certain unchanging smell—if you asked me
what the years smelled like I'd say,
like *that*—and someone besides a mother demanding discipline).

Or is it Reverend Slate who dares
to dream a world wholly immeasurable,
visible to no one's eye, not even his own
though he's given his life to the search?

The more practical, the more useful, hard and rough
the daily men of Oxford, the softer he seems, Sundays, the smoother
and whiter those hands gripping the pulpit—

in this low, tree-shadowed village a glimpse of sky
to me, in the heat of the day a long cool drink,
to others (Chip and Fry, two among many)
a laughingstock, a lily.

Remember the flood? Oh, Nan—remember the vicious water
licking at the bridge, how we watched from the shore
the furious river seething and boiling, and the dogs
raving, running in circles? You said they were like wind-up toys.
And then it fell back, as if it had changed
its mind; it became itself so quickly, bobbing and shaking, shiny again.
We were disappointed—we had braced for a showdown.

Or the day we buried grandmother Rule, who hadn't spoken
out loud for fifteen years, though my mother always
understood her, and the perfect double rainbow circled the graveyard
like an echo. There was no way to be sorrow-struck
because she was with us still, apparently, twice, in full color,
only happier.

I poke and prod and both my children laugh at what I am sure they must
    remember—
the fire that ate up Bishop's barn and blew down the hill right at us
while their father wet the house down and they passed the buckets
like everyone else? The snow days, cozy
in the lee of the woodstove, picturing the darkened school
chill and deserted, like something shunned?

The conversations about war. Dying. Friendship.
The Sunday mornings under the covers tickling their dad,
bringing me Mother's Day on a tray with a single sweet-breathed
rose. ("It cost two dollars!" Chip whispered,
a loving warning.)

            No, no, they tell me now. Or: Sort of,
the snow days, of course. Delicious. The cocoa.
(They remember food better than anything.) The sweet corn. The pizza

that always burned the roofs of their mouths.
Nasturtium leaves and violets in sugar. Italian ice.

Chip says, But remember the sandpit, and the June bugs
bumping around like drunk drivers, they used to scare me so I couldn't
      sleep.
And the truck that sank in the muck of Skowie Pond
and we swam out to see if the driver was in it? The frogs
we smashed on the rocks, me and Troy? I don't know why we did that.

And Nan—all of it private, all of it
quiet, the cakewalk she won and then, running home, how she
dropped the cake. Making a dress
of purple cotton and sewing the arm to the collar. She's sure
I abandoned her one day at Greta Tomkins's house,
late afternoon and I didn't come and didn't come and dark fell
and the dinner plates came out but she was too embarrassed to call, and
      then she knew
finally, surely, she wasn't really our daughter.

I don't remember leaving her that way. Ever.
Not true, I tell her. No way. True,
she swears. Her truth glowers
at my truth, and there is no referee. I try
a different tack: But how can you not—and she says, pushing
her lip out, stubborn—Because I don't.

They have forgotten the childhoods we had
together, they remember only their own. When we finish and clear the
      table,
Nan says, Mother, why are you crying? Please don't

cry. Why does it matter? Don't you think
we love you? She is looking a little alarmed.

I shake my head, pretend to laugh, pour more tea, slop over the rim.
Because it was my life, darling. Because
I thought we were here together,
but I see there's no such thing. It's no news they've earned
their own lives. A momentary anger.
I press a napkin to the saucer.
It wasn't a waste, I caution myself. It wasn't,
and can't believe my selfishness. No leaves in the bottom of a cup
with tea bags, I laugh. No fair, no
fortunes. And they call this progress!

I hate to think how we make do: it's me and Prance the cat.
I love the little cat—that's not the point.

But all the warmth a woman wants
seems to be less the work of piled-up quilts,

let alone husbands whose legs entangle ours,
than the weight of the curve, the fur, the flick of whiskers

humped rumbling in the middle of the arctic bed.
Nothing's more loyal, more quiet, more contented

than this smallest lover, this tender sac of bones and blood,
this delicate listening head.

Once a minister who lived in this house went out
to search for his wife, who had vanished just before midnight,
and found her, naked, sitting in the branches of a maple
at the top of the sloping meadow.
"I am leaving the kingdom of God," she told him without regret,
"for the kingdom of man."

"And for that you have removed your gown?"
he asked, and when he surveyed the moonlit meadow
there on the crown of the hill, he found
the blacksmith's son hiding in a bush,
a small man—a boy, really—on whose narrow shoulders
the world suddenly lay, placed there by a woman.

I read this in the journal we found in the attic—
how the husband called himself a widower from that night forward.
I wanted to be the woman, so decisive, who turned her breasts
up to the moon to be blessed, and then be done forever
with blessing. But I could imagine and maybe pity, for all our sakes,
the innocent who found himself and his urgent body
caught in that trap. The boy who envied the man he'd cuckolded,
the one who walked down the hill set free.

Fry says I'm like a baby doctor—
I deliver whatever I must.

Last week I slid into a hundred mailboxes
the shiny high-colored face of a tyrant who could pass

for an ordinary man. Today, again and again
and yet again, a man so rich he could buy New York.

I don't suppose it matters much who sells
those magazines, fame is its own subject.

But some folks have to live on anonymous mail,
a diet of air and water.

BOX HOLDER's starving to death on Bartram Road.
OCCUPANT's thirsty on Old Town Pike, but nobody's sending

the solids, the liquids of the personal,
the sweet particular, the grit and heaviness of a name.

SUBSCRIBER holds *Time* in his hands, an ad, a plea
for a contribution, the photo of this week's missing child and the date

she was last seen. He is the tree who falls in the forest
with no one to hear. Is he—who will answer?—
Is he there?

Now that there's nothing to do but keep the graves—
she weeds, she picks the pebbles off—
my mother's begun her long unraveling, her disappearance.

Endless the empty places where the thread's
slipped out of the weave. Each loss, each question,
means another hole: *Where are we now?*
Who's that in the hall? When's summer?
Are those my saddle shoes? My hairpins? Where's the cat? I think
she thinks the cat's my father, soft when she loves him,
the dog when she's angry. Then his barking
disturbs her. She shouts at him viciously, using his name:
Be quiet, Frank, be quiet for once
or go sleep in the barn with the babies!

Anita said, when you finally stop
bleeding, your life begins. (Myself,
I thought it was ending.) But that's neither here nor there:

she's disappeared. We worried about abduction
but there weren't any hints. We thought anger,
enough to drive her off, but she wasn't angry to the naked eye.

A man? we asked of each other, unbelieving. A whole new life?
Her Jack is running round in circles, keeping busy.
He printed a hundred of her smiling face,

put them on every post and tree, as if
in a town this size everyone wasn't already looking,
whispering, praying. "Maybe she went with the *ladies*,"

Fry says, smarmy. Maybe she's in the woods,
my friends and I are thinking, under a swell of leaves,
her secrets in the hand that holds the pearl revolver

that's missing with her. Her children are little stones of silence,
her parents are far beyond tears, beyond recognition,
and I've been thinking, Anita, please,

give us a hint: animal, vegetable, mineral? Are you living
in a lair? Planting and burgeoning? Still
as an outcropping? If you won't tell,

we'll have to dream you into whatever we need.
We won't stop till you're taller, thinner, smart as a city lawyer.
The deeper we're stuck, the more we envy and fear for you.
Imagining is not daring. Wishing is not going somewhere.

When they say, "The bottom's fallen out,"
what they mean is Fry's face gone tight as shoe leather
each time he opens the envelope that might
have the pink slip in it.
(And the executioner hides
behind the slip—he'd never dare walk in and deliver,
man to man, the fatal tap on the shoulder.)

That's ruined better men than mine.
I hear their wives complain how they used to be up to greet the birds
but now they can't get out of bed of a morning.
The nest is fouled and what can I offer
but kitchen comfort? The day that slip, pink as a rose,
flutters out of his envelope, Fry's gone
till midnight and I'm no good for anything. (Payday: I know
before I know.) He staggers home, dwindled to half his size
before he's slept on it a single night,
says in a gutted voice "They lowered the boom"

and I see it, realer than real: the wrecking ball
that plummets from the plant roof straight as a shot,
his name on its side in blood-red letters: **FRY, old man,
what can we say? The goddam bottom's fallen out.**

Three months into Nothing To Do,
I asked if he wanted my mail route: You
drive, I said, I'll clean some houses,
shake the mothballs off my waitress gear—easier
to slip me in some little space, a mouse
through a hole in the wall, than you.
I was being cheerful,
I wanted to save his battered face,
but he shouted *No!*

That was the only time
I ever thought he was going to hit me, this husband of mine, and,
    do you know,
I can't think why. Which of us
was he hurt for? Both of us desperate, but differently,
was it offering women's work—as if men don't
deliver the mail—or *my* work, my gift
of something he didn't want to need
but needed,
that shamed him so?

Good as they get, I think—a fine feisty girl
with early laugh lines, a pure
soprano for the choir, a tendency to thicken a little
a little too soon—my son's wife's only fault is
she was born a stranger, and grew up
to seduce my son.

I was down on my knees
sweetening the soil with the edge of my trowel
when Michelle ran up in her sweats and leaned across the fence.
(She calls me Cora, which I don't much like,
but I couldn't take Mother from someone else's daughter.)
And we nibbled and chewed
and after the appetizers the main course came: Already
he's out with the boys too many nights. Already
throwing the "blank-blank" dishtowel across the kitchen.
He's thinking maybe he'll take a little trip with his buddies,
camp in the woods without women. We can imagine: Pee
for distance. Belch without apology. Bond.

It didn't take long, did it. Oh, what did you love
in him first, I ask her, reaching back into myself.
He can be gentle, Chip can, when he chooses.
He can be funny, he brings the sweetest gifts, he's fierce as a pit bull
defending his own. "Or not,"
she says. "We're in a not phase now." Michelle
works at the day care: "The way you talk about two-year-olds,"
she laughs, and the lines fan out around her eyes
like the whiskers of a cat. I don't want to see it,

the pale girl in her flowered nightie, freckled,
leaving her curlers out, her skin cream off, so she won't

disgust him, waiting in a clench on the flowered bed,
all her nonchalance gone, her plan to be
indifferent. Her husband standing at the window studying the dark,
his back to his wife, to the furniture
that owns them.
She giving quietly, he quietly refusing.
Finally, fat with tears, she lies down on her side, on top
of the sheet. She's asleep
before he turns the bedside light out, before he climbs in beside her.

She isn't mine, she's someone else's daughter.
He's my son. She shouldn't ask me to see this.

Maybe he wakes her. Maybe she's surprised
and grins in the dark, over his warm shoulder.
Maybe she blesses the man he is,
the man he could become.

Thicker, more tapered,
shaped for a different body that leaks the same old way,
it's still a diaper.

She's still, however
much ashamed, my mother.

This is the day
(I wipe my eyes on my rolled-up sleeve and smile)
before the end of days.

A TV crew is sucking Oxford to it
like nails to a magnet. We are to be
disguised as what we are: If village houses
favor tubs of petunias, so be it, here come a dozen
fat petunia pots, crammed to bursting, wheels of photogenic red and
   purple.
If the Scotts happen to fly a flag beside their door on Main Street,
a dozen houses this perfect morning
festoon themselves with rented flags. I'm sure
they're praying for a wind, everything's quainter
with a ripple. Maybe they'll bring in
a wind machine. Money floats on the air like pollen.

Me they follow. They watch me sort and pack my mail
(nobody helps me lug it to the car),
they smile at my steering wheel on the curb side,
nod when I tug the first box open, push down the flag with the side of
   my hand,
they smile and shout and eavesdrop on my conversations
with—"What do you call them, clients? Customers?" somebody asks,
   as if that's funny. "You stand here"
is the refrain of the day, and everybody's grateful and obedient
as children. Nathan Bing smooths his thinning hair,
wipes the shine from his ample nose, practices
a conspirator's smile I've never seen. I'm getting mad,

I feel my whole face closing down. They dangle
a microphone over us the way a bluebird
buzzes a cat. "Just talk
the way you always talk," the director shouts
and his little assistant in blue jeans writes on her clipboard.

Nathan tells me to have a nice day, bright as a cheerleader. Here's
where I look sick. I try to ignore them.
Mail Woman is a heroine, like Wonder Woman, I don't play
and can't fake. I glower and the little assistant mutters to her boss,
"*She's* a dead one."
I've sent us straight to the cutting-room floor. Poor Nathan,
his fifteen seconds of fame and I've jinxed them!

The thing is, I want to make a chorus line
of the men laid off at the plant this winter without warning.
I want a close-up of the real estate agent
when she pounds another FOR SALE sign into the ground.
I'm not in the mood for cute or sweet or safe right now,
though there'll still be plenty of each in Oxford the day the world ends.

The thing is, I don't want Fry, home with the tube
and a bottle of Lite, to change channels and see his wife, bare-faced,
loving her job this much, gunning the motor, singing.
winding her way uphill and down like the unbreakable thread
I surely am—
my father's daughter—
that helps to hold this town together.

The two of them approach, so slow
you almost fall asleep between the raising
of the walker and the lowering,
the raising and lowering, the jangle like a pocketful of keys
and the steady ka-chunk of the metal cage, its meek monster footstep.
But it keeps on coming. Age
and her daughter are squeezing the bread,
bagging Golden Delicious, discussing the roast. Amiable.
Patience rises from their skins like a perfume. I watch them coming,

going, I, Cora, whose impatience, today, rises like a stench
in my own nostrils. Tender the way their necks are identical, bent
at the same blunt angle, over the cod on sale—
the mother, Annie Lofts, and the daughter,
my old friend Tara.
Tara the daughter, this is, not Tara the lover.

But maybe loving's a habit that feeds itself, like milk
when you're nursing—don't use it,
lose it. The more the baby sucks the more
you have to give it. (The opposite of money!) And Tara's love,
Lord knows it stays
accessible. Tara in her shorts and lavender tube top, sinewy, now, as a
        chicken,
calf muscles tight over dangerous heels,
leads her nearly-transparent mother
to the checkout, smiling like a saint.
(Be fair: that's not a smile for us.)

                    Nobody ever said
virtue was consistent, did they, or could be measured
like the price of the hamburger in my basket. I, for instance,

a good girl, known to be
just a touch too good, or at least not loose
in the love department, suffered a little failure of that love,
a blackout, we might call it, the screws, we might say,
too tight: yelled at my mother this morning
when she said the same thing over
one time too many (a thing I didn't want to hear
even the first time).
I wish I could think of a punishment,
I keep remembering how Miss Rembar (seventh grade) truly believed
that soap in the mouth went bubbling
straight to our nasty souls. She'd go to the sink behind us
and watch while we scrubbed and rinsed and nearly wrung our teeth
as if our words were underwear. Then she hung us out to dry.

Annie Lofts clatters to the door and, arms full, Tara
turns to me and smiles: *Still here? I do this better
than you?* Fondling a cabbage, foolish,
I miss her, miss my mother—miss
myself, long gone. Her smile nearly forgives me. *Cora,*
I think it says. *Look at us, child.
Look at the two of us! Aren't we in the soup
together.*

Mortgage the house,
   my city cousin says,
      helpful as poison.

Sell off the sweet acres
   across the brook?
      But no one is buying now,

no one is gathering in:
   The whole world's selling its birthright.
      Trying to. Failing.

We look for our place
   on the TV graphs.
      The dark bar's gain, the pale one loss.

Loss is leading. Fry says if he must,
   he'll hunt our meat.
      I'm ready to eat red beans and rice—

Look on the healthy side, I'll lose some weight!
   Hold tight, he says. Who knows,
      maybe I'll pull my ski mask over my eyes

and rob the Quickie Mart. Don't joke like that,
   I say, but his eyes are fierce
      and I think, It does start somewhere.

Somebody's running out of faith and choices,
   someone like Fry, who didn't ask for this,
      before he opens fire.

Rumor grows green and thick as a lawnful of clover.
The season's changed but Anita Stryk goes right on being missing.

If you care to listen to speculation,
she's raising twins in Carolina,
she died on the abortionist's table, screaming
her children's names. Her husband did her in
for her insurance. She's living (known as Nita)
with a black musician, singing in nightclubs
in her scanties.

Dear Oxford, here's a letter:

Friends:

I deliver the mail to the Stryks. Never a word
from Anita. But the bills, the dunning letters
are falling like acid rain on Jack Stryk's head. The bank writes him so
    often
their envelopes singe my sorting hand. Today
I brought a little message from Bankruptcy Court—I could almost
hear it ticking. Gossip or not, here in the bright blue mailbox,
sealed and stamped, are the reasons she's gone:
I don't know where she is, his loving wife,
but I know she saw the explosion coming and her house on fire,
and—clothes on her back and nothing in her hands, poor woman,
not even her children—ran for her own dear ruined life.

Everyone's lives have begun to look alike.
Jeanine Derbyfield, her hair still thick and red as a fox's,
who never said a willing word to me in school—
Jeanine-the-jock, all muscle, all desperate winner, who mocked
the rest of us for our books, our sagging gym suits, our old-lady
legs—sits in the waiting room with her mother

who looks like my mother in her white lace cap of hair,
dozing, smiling at her knees,
and we finally talk, quietly, Jeanine and I,
below the threshold of their blasted hearing.

I swear, the deeper into the muck and muddle of our particulars—
the insulin shots, the weddings, wills,
douches and rhododendrons, the pills and potato bugs, the bankruptcies
and valedictorians and drop-outs, the picnics and teapots and wakes—
the farther away we get.

                              No, the higher up. I feel like a pilot
flying over the tiny, separate plots of our lives,
I see how the shapes we've worked so hard at carving out and cultivating
to look like no one else's begin to resemble each other. At fifteen thousand
      feet,
they blend, their borders run together, vague, finally invisible.

From here, in fact, the plots become identical—Lord, those deep,
dark rectangles! Figures mill around for a while
like ants. Later, someone tucks them under a quilt of grass
and the hillside goes on again, uninterrupted.

Jeanine, holding her mother's boneless hand, must see it too: When
      someone
carves a name on a stone,
that's how we'll know it's ours.

The sun rises on another chance.
Fry buttons his jacket, unbuttons it,
curses the beers of yesteryear
when he didn't have to worry where they went,
or shave close for some stranger.

He's seeing himself with the stranger's eyes, how could he not,
and doesn't like the sight. He sits in a slump,
I'll bet, a Don't-expect-me-to-love-you
sulk, and the interview goes flat, like a tire
pierced by a nail. He rides home raging,

bare rim slapping the ground. Everything he knows
is disappearing—how fast those roots wither in air,
like a ripped-out vine! Nathan, Pat, and now Tim's joined them,
lean on Fry's pickup at noon, and spit and make large motions

of vengeance. Through the open kitchen window
I hear Fry's dream: *the whole plant up in flames—*
he shakes his head to dislodge it—*the pumpers frozen to the spot*
while the fire whistle moans and howls,
and no survivors, not even their friends
who kept their jobs.

Especially their friends.

And now, and now,
Salvation, out of the blue.

A sure thing if you want it.
Say the word, friend.
Hourly's good. Benefits
so deep you'll want to get sick
just to see them go to work.

Oxford, you can visit weekends.
You can keep your friends.
Hell, you can keep your garden!
A couple of hours, terrific highway,
no two-lane. A snap. Over the mountain.
Fry. We need good men. Strong. Quick.
You pass it up,
never again.
Never again.
Damn lucky.
Shake?

It was the eagerness that caught him.
The being courted.
I watched the blood rush to his cheeks.
He was like a lover spurned too many times,
finally loved back. Needed.
He drank their reassurance like a drug.
He let them plead.

What could I hold against it?

> The little wife?
> They love it here—
> Shopping. Bunch of churches.
> A lake. Look at the lake!
> She swim, your wife?

Only my life.

I can't say I didn't cry for a week,
publicly, privately, cry such tears
I thought the mulch would turn to mud
around my flowers' ankles.

He didn't want to do it to me.
He didn't deserve to suffer my anger,
and I didn't want to kill him with it.
But I told him he could shoot me with less pain.

I saw my mother go into the ground without me.
My son's unborn children will hide when they see me coming.
I'll forget the names of my first friends.
I won't know whose sweet white house is whose,

their dogs will snarl when I stop to talk to them,
their mailboxes locked against my hand.
And won't they bury me outside the graveyard fence, out in the meadow
where the grass grows rank and wild?

I think you have one life, I told him, sorry to say it.
You cup your hands and drink it deep,
or you pour it out on strange ground
like so much spilled water.

All these years, through many colors, it's been the Carty place
    (CHAS. CARTY 1844).
His children added and cobbled on and changed the roofline, all those
    handy sons
without self-consciousness, working together bare-chested, carving it into
    shapes

faint as the memory of their names (Chas. Jr., Thomas, Leland, Payne,
    and the wives
Polly, Elviria, Mary and none for the bachelor Payne). Now that our own
    little changes
are forever finished, our children come to it as visitors—glad to be free
    of it, missing it,
taking it for granted. It can't hold them but still it's theirs, or meant to
    be.

Now that we've packed those good years and terrible years in boxes too
    large to be lifted,
shearing ourselves from it violently, giving over the familiar turn in the
    stairs,
the fireplace Fry built with stones from the brook, this cellar whose shelves
sag under the weight of my bell jars, my salty amethysts, my sweetest
    rubies,

now that it's past tense, someone else's, the house will
take our name. That's how they do it, you know: wait till you're gone.
    Over the mountain
in a five-year-old ranch constructed from toothpicks and covered with
    pale yellow siding,
we'll feel it, shaken, the first time anyone calls it THE FRY PLACE:

Who, we will ask, is walking on our graves?

Notes for the move:

A box (not a cage!) for Prance-the-cat.

Take cuttings (in earth, if there's time). Must have.

Instead of a yard sale, give gifts. Remember who's liked what.
Tell friends not to *bring* gifts—no new clutter!

Break in new nurse for Mother. Give her whatever she asks.

Visit the graves. Father's greens are finally catching. Grandmother Rule's
needs clearing. No hired hands to keep them tended—
will do it when I visit.

And Joanie—poor Joanie's stone (*Dear wife and mother*) doesn't tell
how she rushed to get here, already gone to ashes.

Goodbye to Reverend Slate. Ask him for prayers. (Fry doesn't get any.)

An hour for the dump. Goodbye to Horace, dump-man,
and his muddy pitchfork. Build in time
to sway at the edge of the pit—It used to be the devil's fire,
all orange rinds, cereal boxes, pill bottles, diapers,
silver foil and gold, cough drops, condoms,
everything swirled together, all of Oxford public, private,
turned to smoke more sweet than you'd imagine.
Now fire's against the law they plow it
under—it is what it is now, not very pretty.

Return cookbooks to Fran. Her baby's colicky, she's had no sleep
for weeks. A child of technology, she plays the dryer, the vacuum,

to comfort him with a rumble. (When the Lord smiled on her womb
at last, it was a crooked smile.)

Party at the P.O. Will let them see my tears. (Why not?)
The cake will be too rich, made by somebody patient,
roses and all. I'll never have time to learn
that flick of the wrist for sugar roses.

Close bank account. Bitterness, but not for the teller
(who went to school with Chip!). Save some cake to sweeten
nasty mouth after the closing signature.
When I was ten we banked a quarter once a week.
Now, *that* was money!

The long drive home, a last time:

Fry made love to me in the fine spray of the waterfall once, behind it,
where the beavers live. Would he remember? What's a memory worth?

Poor Tatty, Dickie's aunt, lived in rubble in that house
till they pulled her out, scratching, stinking.

Beech forked by lightning. Gorgeous wood exposed, like white fat flesh.

Chip went courting here when he and Jane Pratt were eleven.
She told her mother he bit her on the ear. He asked,
"Isn't that how you kiss if it's not your sister?"

Anita's house. Still mourning the mystery—she seems
to be vanished forever. *Anita, can you hear me? We're vanishing too.*

Park on the far side of the house, near the brook. The moving truck
will dig its ruts a mile deep in the driveway.
A spiteful signature, that double ditch, for the new owners—
gouge like a mark of anger.

My mother has done with me. She doesn't understand "Goodbye-
we'll-see-you-soon." Like a traffic light, it's only Yes. No.
Stop. Go. Tears. Mine. Hers. "So,
aren't you leaving?" she asks, impatient. "Why are you still here?"

Yes, I say. Yes, we're going. Soon, dear. When I'm able.
I can't say goodbye or even try to name
my losses, chimney, pinecone, cellar hole,
gas pump, columbine tangled in the berry brakes. Five hundred names.
But I say to myself, Nobody wants you dead, Cora. Nobody
even wants you sad or robbed. Snipers,
stalkers, soldiers patrol the world, wishing evil
to strangers. Nobody needs your fuss.
There's self-respect in going quietly.

My father said (and more than once), *Choice rots the bones.*
He didn't say what happens to *No choice left,*
or when to cut your losses.
I see those prairie schooners setting sail, and some from here,
into the tall grass; the grass, quietly parted,
closing like water behind their wake. And immigrants
toting their quilts and pillows, their woks, their babies,

boat people, black-clothed families stuffed into steerage, breathless,
the new world coming toward them like a meteor, ungently.
How many people have this much choice? I see us from a distance.
Fry, oh Fry, I know: *It could be worse.*

Trapper is breathing in my ear. Prance, curled like a snake,
sleeps on, not in, his box. We crest the hill, the car so full
we surely can't see behind us, lampshades piled
on pillows piled on the rim of the swaying ficus.
Then I suppose we're Prance's cousins, beginning our second life.
There's nowhere to look but forward.

Printed in the USA
CPSIA information can be obtained
at www.ICGtesting.com
LVHW091134150724
785511LV00001B/130

9 780374 524432